The secrets of success in coaching

Books that make you better

Books that make you better. That make you *be* better,
do better, *feel* better. Whether you want to upgrade
your personal skills or change your job, whether you
want to improve your managerial style, become
a more powerful communicator, or be stimulated
and inspired as you work.

Prentice Hall Business is leading the field with a new
breed of skills, careers and development books. Books
that are a cut above the mainstream – in topic, content
and delivery – with an edge and verve that will make
you better, with less effort.

Books that are as sharp and smart as you are.

Prentice Hall Business.
We work harder – so you don't have to.

For more details on products, and to contact us, visit
www.pearsoned.co.uk

The secrets of success in coaching

12 ways to excel as a coach

Mick Cope

**Prentice Hall
Business**
is an imprint of

Harlow, England • London • New York • Boston • San Francisco • Toronto
Sydney • Tokyo • Singapore • Hong Kong • Seoul • Taipei • New Delhi
Cape Town • Madrid • Mexico City • Amsterdam • Munich • Paris • Milan

PEARSON EDUCATION LIMITED

Edinburgh Gate
Harlow CM20 2JE
Tel: +44 (0)1279 623623
Fax: +44 (0)1279 431059
Website: www.pearsoned.co.uk

First published in Great Britain in 2010

© Pearson Education Limited 2010

The right of Mick Cope to be identified as author of this work has been asserted by
him in accordance with the Copyright, Designs and Patents Act 1988.

Pearson Education is not responsible for the content of third party internet sites.

ISBN: 978-0-273-73184-9

British Library Cataloguing-in-Publication Data
A catalogue record for this book is available from the British Library

Library of Congress Cataloguing-in-Publication Data
A catalog record for this book is available from the Library of Congress

10 9 8 7 6 5 4 3 2 1
14 13 12 11 10

Text design by Sue Lamble
Typeset in 10 pt Iowan Old Style by 30
Printed in Great Britain by Henry Ling Ltd., at the Dorset Press, Dorchester, Dorset

Contents

About the author

MICK COPE is founder of WizOz – an organisation that seeks to help people and businesses optimise their potential. Mick offers a range of different products and services, all of which are based around the ideas outlined in his books. More information on these can be found on his website, www.mickcope.co.uk.

As an author he has published seven books: *Leading the Organisation to Learn*, *Seven Cs of Consulting*, *Know your value? Value what you know*, *Lead Yourself*, *Float-You*, *Personal Networking* and *7Cs of Coaching*.

He has a number of goals in life, the simple one being to live a life of personal freedom where he is able to think, feel and behave according to his values and not succumb to the demands of others. The more challenging one is to help 1000 people achieve the same in their life.

He would love any feedback on any concepts offered in this book. Contact him at mickcope@btinternet.com.

Acknowledgements

Huge thanks to the commune (Ffyona, Lin, Marc, Sam and Stu) for keeping my feet on the ground and always offering a warm and welcoming place to chew the fat. Don't forget Cornwall – I love it.

Thanks

Mick

Introduction

COACHING IS A POWERFUL TOOL that can have a profound impact on someone's personal and professional life. But coaching can only really be successful when the coach:

- is truly competent in their work
- follows a client centric-coaching approach
- has a deep ethical sense of responsibility
- seeks to help the client deliver change that is of value and sustainable.

An excellent coach can be likened to a grizzled old plumber who you call out when your heating and water systems have failed. After a few questions, a couple of taps on the water pipes and a quick look at the boiler, they can immediately diagnose and resolve the problem. What to a layperson can seem like a high cost for an apparently simple action is actually of immense value, because you are paying for the years and years of experience that they are able to deliver in a single moment.

In *The Secrets of Success in Coaching*, I want to share with you my years of coaching experience to help you become a highly successful and competent coach. Whether you already are, or are hoping to be, a life coach, a performance coach, an executive coach, a manager who coaches a team or any other kind of coach, this book will give you a clear set of coaching tools to help you ensure that every one of your client relationships is successful and the changes you help them make are sustainable.

there is no short cut to becoming a truly excellent coach

I won't ask you to change your current coaching practice; the advice I offer here is designed to enrich what you already do, not challenge it. Be prepared for some hard work though – there is no short cut to becoming a truly excellent coach and it will take time, patience and effort. But if you put into practice the 'secrets' in this book, you'll be well on your way to becoming a great coach.

Using tried-and-tested coaching techniques and tools, this book will offer you the following:

◆ A core set of techniques broken down in sections – so you can read the chapter and apply the idea immediately with your client.

◆ A series of killer apps – things that you need to do to ensure that your client relationships are successful and sustainable.

◆ A range of simple but powerful coaching questions that will help you to apply the ideas immediately.

◆ A tool kit that you can share with your clients – if you are both working from the same coaching map then working together will be made easier immediately.

◆ A way of working that will complement your current style of coaching rather than asking you to change how you work.

◆ Solutions to help you move forward with your client, if you ever feel you are stuck.

If you are just starting your coaching career or looking for new skills and tips to take a big leap forward, this book has been designed to help you move from where you are now to where you want to be.

How to use this book

My best advice is not to read the book in one go and try all the ideas. Rather, read one of the twelve chapters, reflect on it and try to understand what it means to you and how you can use it. You don't need to start with the first idea in the book – just find one that looks interesting and you think might be fun to try out.

You'll find a set of coaching questions in the chapters. Try to think about how the questions will fit your natural style and then adapt them to suit you as you see fit. Once you've tried some of them out, ask yourself:

◆ How did I plan to use the idea and questions?

◆ How did it turn out?

◆ What did I like and what didn't I like?

◆ Would I change anything when I use it next time?

◆ When can I next try out the idea and revised questions with a client?

You'll also find models in each chapter. If you try a new model each week, over a couple of months you will have added significantly to your armory as a coach.

Have fun with each chapter, and remember that there is no *right* way to coach, there is just *your* way – and *The Secrets of Success in Coaching* will help you be the very best coach you can be.

there is no right *way to coach, there is just* your *way*

1

Creating the perfect coach/client relationship

Find the right client – you can't coach someone who doesn't want to change

AS A COACH YOU CAN USE a certain set of ideas, philosophies and techniques that can and will make a difference to people – BUT only if they want to make a difference to themselves.

As a coach you must ask if a person really wants to be coached: do they really want to change and do they really want the change to last? So many people say they want some-thing – but what they actually want is the easy way to get there without putting the effort in. Real personal change and real coaching is about finding clients who are serious about themselves, their change and the service they want from the coach.

ask if a person really wants to be coached

Below are three pillars that underpin the delivery of successful and sustainable coaching. These three pillars support the whole engagement process, namely the need to ensure that the client is tuned in to the ideas of invitation, intent and a desire for independence.

- **Invitation** – You must respect the fact that you can only be invited to help someone help themselves. All personal change is about personal choice and this must be through invitation rather than imposition. In the situation where the manager or coach chooses to 'coach' someone because 'they need it', this is not coaching – this is performance management.

- **Intent** – Your goal is to test and ensure that the client has fully committed to realising a sustainable change before entering into a partnership. If the engagement commences without clear intent, then it will probably fail to deliver sustainable value. It may deliver a short-term change, but the chances of realising a sustainable benefit will be suspect.

- **Independence** – Your primary role must be to help the client fly solo at the end of the engagement. You need to be really confident that the client is able to self-sustain their change and not be reliant on you for tangible or intangible support. You must help make the client aware that there will come a point when the dependency will be cut and they will have to be confident of standing on their own.

As a coach you are there to help the client deliver value through sustainable change – not to do it for them. But this leads to the question: do they want to change or, like so many people who try to change, do they just *want to want to*?

Separate those who will from those who won't

In essence, you need to identify those who can and want to change, as opposed to those who won't or can't. This seemingly simple piece of advice holds the key to successful coaching and development programmes.

The simple approach below allows you to assess whether your client is serious about change – and will help you decide whether or not you can help them.

identify those who can and want to change

Clients tend to fall into one of the following five 'P' categories where change is concerned.

◆ **Players** – these are clients who are up for the change. They want to get on the pitch and play the game as soon as possible. They are passionate about being successful and also about ensuring that their change will stick and they'll not revert to old ways. It is clearly at the top of their list of personal priorities and this is self-evident in how they manage any pre-work and homework. If they are serious players then they will be serious about investing time and energy in the process.

◆ **Participants** – they will be involved in the coaching journey and there is clear evidence of their willingness to make the investment. The difference between the participant and the player is that for the participant it is not at the top of their list. Like the observer at a sports match, they will enthuse for one day a week and be an active supporter – but the player on the pitch lives and breathes it every day. The participant is not a bad client, but it is interesting to ask what you will have to do to help them step up to the player level and make it really important.

◆ **Passengers** – this might be the channel flicker. They have come into the coaching relationship because it seemed like a good idea at the time, but there isn't a huge amount of passion. As such the next bright shiny thing that comes along could take their attention and they will be off.

◆ **Prisoners** – this client has been sent by their boss, partner or someone in their life who exerts influence over their choices. They will attend physically but there is little chance that they will engage at a head or heart level. They will go through the motions, forget to do any homework and often cancel appointments at the last minute. Not a good option and in most cases their attitude needs to be challenged at the outset. For me, if the client isn't prepared to change their attitude then I tend to change the client. My goal is to opt to work with people who choose to work with me.

◆ **Protesters** – these are the clients who have been sent to you to be 'fixed' or 'sorted out'. The difference between the protestor and the prisoner is that the protester is voicing the things that the prisoner is thinking. So the coaching often becomes a battleground. In effect it isn't coaching – it is full-blown performance management and needs to be recognised as such.

> ## Coaching questions
>
> At the first coaching session, you need to identify which
> category your client fits into. The best way to do this is
> through a set of focused questions. The questions below can
> be used to gauge your client's category.
>
> ◆ Why are you here?
>
> ◆ What do you want to achieve?
>
> ◆ What have you heard about the coaching?
>
> ◆ What do you plan to do at the end of the coaching?
>
> ◆ Have you completed any pre-work?
>
> ◆ Do you see value in the coaching?
>
> ◆ Do you feel free to pull out if the coaching is not seen to
>   add value?
>
> ◆ What is your previous experience of being coached?

Be warned, though, your client might not be used to being
challenged about their intent, especially if someone else has
put them forward for coaching, so you will need to tread
carefully. However, not doing this makes you complicit in
any failure to deliver the final outcome. Discussing these
issues at the early stage of the coaching cycle can seem challenging, but, I would argue, brushing the chances of a failed
outcome under the carpet and assuming that all will be fine
will present greater challenges later on.

2

Set the scene

WHEN YOU ARE SATISFIED that your client falls into the right 'P' category described in Chapter 1, you need to ensure other factors are right for the coaching relationship to be successful. Like a great film, book or play, the first scene is there to help contextualise the situation, identify who the players are and also signal the way forward. Coaching is no different – in the early stages you need to set the scene with the client and make sure that all the factors are in place to ensure that a successful outcome can be achieved.

In the first meeting you need to understand why your client wants the coaching to take place, and you need to assess whether it can be delivered and whether you believe you can help. There are five key factors you can test that will help you to do this:

- Subjective – Is the change about them or someone else?
- Singular – Are they trying to change too many things at once?

◆ Small – Is it small enough to be managed in a limited time frame?

◆ Specific – Is it measurable?

◆ Significant – Is it important enough to give some leverage and make a difference?

You may well find that your client wants to address an issue that can't be resolved without a significant investment in time and motivation. There is often a commonly held belief by clients that personal change can be fixed quickly and easily with the help of a good coach. Personal change, however, in most cases, takes time and, some argue, making it stick is rare. Just think about how many people will be at a diet club tonight across the country – and how many do you think will actually lose weight? Then consider that same group and ask yourself how many will keep the weight off? Even though they are paying the money and going through the process of seeking to change their life, it is a big challenge and, in many cases, people fail to make it happen.

the viability issue needs to be considered at the outset

People often go through a process where they jump head first into a coaching relationship without asking some pertinent questions about either their readiness to change or the viability of the action they want to take. And it is the viability issue that needs to be considered at the outset of the coaching process. Specifically, is the outcome achievable within the given constraints of the coaching relationship? Successful coaching depends on you testing whether the action is viable *before* the client commits to the programme.

Check if it is a project with legs and will last

You can determine if the client's project stands a good chance of achieving success by working through the five areas outlined below.

Make sure it is about them and not others

This test is designed to ensure that the client can actually effect a change over the problem. This is because so often clients will ask for coaching on the following types of issue:

◆ 'I want to get promoted.'

◆ 'I want people to like me.'

◆ 'I am not happy with the environment.'

The problem with these topics is that the factor that needs to change is actually beyond the control of the client. It is like saying, 'I am fed up with the bad weather and I want it to change.' My being upset is my response to external stimuli – and although you can change how you feel, you have no power to change the weather. So the client topic focus needs to be from a subjective rather than objective basis.

Listen to the language the client uses to describe the problem. There is a spread that ranges from objective to subjective.

◆ 'It' – This is where the client describes the problem in terms of something that is out there. This can often be seen when people talk about a problem with the 'system' or 'culture', all aspects that are unlikely to be under the control of the client.

- ◆ **'They'** – This is classically where the client talks about other people as the problem, such as the senior managers, the other team or the customers.

- ◆ **'We'** – In this case the client talks about problems within their team. This might be raising motivational issues, gripes within the team or general performance problems.

- ◆ **'You'** – In this case the client talks about one other person as being the issue. This might be due to relationship breakdown, different working styles or just wanting the other person to change their behaviour.

Where coaching topics are described using any of these four words, in most cases it will fail to deliver any real sustainable benefits. This is because the focus is on trying to change something over which the client has little or no control. The client has to accept that the only thing they can change in life is themselves. From this standpoint we should be aiming to get the client to describe their coaching from an 'I' perspective.

- ◆ **'I'** – This is where the client says, 'I want to be become more promotable', 'I want to learn how to build relationships with people', or 'I want to understand how to operate in an environment that is not a natural home for me'.

With this statement you are able to work with the client on here and now issues and help to deal with real and tangible concerns that the client can work on.

One of the things you should look out for is the client's tendency to spin out to the *it, them, you* and *we* language.

This is because this language allows the client not to own the problem. If the client can use objective statements and push the problem outside their sphere of control then they can absolve themselves of responsibility to do something about it. Consider how the person addicted to smoking will blame their mates for offering them a cigarette, how the alcoholic will blame the fact that driving home made them stressed and so they needed a drink, or how the dieter blamed the chocolate company for offering a two-for-one deal. In all the cases the moment you challenge the client to use subjective language, such as 'I chose to have a cigarette – my mates didn't actually make me have one', they have to take responsibility for their actions.

Coaching questions

◆ Is this about changing you or how others perceive you?

◆ Is this topic under your control to resolve?

◆ Can anyone prevent you from making the change?

Focus on just one thing at a time

Once you are sure that the client is making a change that they own and is under their control, the next thing to consider is the extent to which the task is manageable. The key here is to focus on doing one thing right – rather than lots of small things wrong!

focus on doing one thing right

The risk with most coaching topics is that people will oversimplify the problem being addressed. Clients will often use vague statements like, 'I want to be happy ... lose weight

... get rich ... change jobs.' This is akin to saying that someone wants to build a bridge, buy a house or learn to drive. At a high level this outcome is great – but there are a multitude of interconnecting tasks that need to be managed to achieve this and a failure of any one of them can lead to the whole project collapsing.

Often, what looks like a simple personal change process requires a complex range of thoughts, feelings and behaviours that need to be linked and managed. One person's statement of 'I want to get fit' has to encompass how they:

- do more exercise
- eat better
- drink less
- stop smoking.

For the client, trying to manage all these tasks at one time can be a strain; and for the coach, keeping track of the various change activities becomes a major issue in its own right. Successful coaching focuses on one thing at one time and seeks to get this delivered in isolation. Once this is locked in then the client can move to the next change and so on. A series of building blocks grows over time and almost creates a compound effect as the interlinking change outcomes mutually reinforce and benefit each other.

The difficulty with this approach is that clients can feel that they are not doing enough and try to take on additional changes. This is because there is often a social pressure to do it big, do it now and do something new tomorrow. It is this social pressure to make big changes coupled with the distorted view presented by the media that often suggests that personal change is easy. You should encourage the client to take a more focused and realistic view of the coaching topic and restrain any tendency to try to 'boil the ocean'.

With this approach there will be a much greater chance of success. Because all of the energy is focused on just one change then the problems of distraction and complication tend to be removed from the equation. Success breeds success. Think about the smoker who has decided to give up cigarettes. If they have already tried five times before and failed to sustain the change, their thinking will naturally be one of fixing the failure. This isn't a great place to start from as it drives a lack of belief in their ability to change. If they enter the change having just successfully completed a previous goal, the positive spirit can only help them enter the new change with a belief in their chances of success. An excellent coach is in the business of helping the client create sustainable successes rather than short-lived solutions.

success breeds success

Your role in helping to make this happen is threefold:

1   Help the client understand that one small, successful and sustainable outcome is worth 10 large failed changes.

2   Ensure that coaching drift doesn't occur as the client begins to see new things they 'could' do; instead make sure that they stick to the knitting and focus on achieving a single sustainable outcome.

3   Always be prepared to challenge the client in case that single change is either the wrong one or there might be a better option. It is far better to stop and change direction than to get locked into a dead-end route.

Always focus on 'just one thing' – it really does make a difference. The simple example being, how do you break a bunch of sticks? The answer being, you don't – you break them one at a time. Together there is just too much resistance to have any impact.

> *Coaching questions*
>
> ◆ How many changes do you think need to be made to achieve the outcome?
>
> ◆ How do you know this is the optimum change to make?
>
> ◆ Once this single change is made, do you know what the next change might be?

Like a good diet – little and often is best

Once you are sure that the client is making a change that they own and it is under their control, the next aspect to consider is the size of the change.

Time and time again the importance of keeping the change small enough to manage but big enough to make a difference proves to be the factor that will help you create excellent outcomes. For a sports coach, it might be helping a golfer shift ever so slightly how they stand, for a footballer, the way they pass, or for a sprinter, how they leave the start. These are micro changes that can deliver major gains in the performance. Please note – small doesn't mean unimportant. The key with this is to maximise the effect of the change topic to help deliver the greatest leverage.

small doesn't mean unimportant

The difficulty with this approach is a risk of 'scope creep'. Often people start with a small and specific change but over time other things get included and it becomes bigger and bigger. So a simple goal to help the client develop even contact with a group when making a presentation can slowly grow into telling a joke to ease the pressure, and then learning how to run a one-hour presentation to deliver to a management board. These are nice aims, but practically it is better to keep each change discrete and so avoid scope creep. Keeping the coaching topic small and simple means just that – it is a much more focused piece of support from you that is designed to deliver a targeted outcome in a limited amount of time with a clear and tangible outcome.

To help this stage of the process you need to really challenge the client to start with a small topic and then keep it small. But at the same time the client needs to test and validate that the action being taken does have the potential to deliver big outcomes and so drive up the potential value to them.

Far too many clients want to leap tall mountains, end world poverty and move from being targeted for redundancy to being marked for promotion in the space of three months! This is not to say that these things are not possible – but for mere mortals like us they take time and energy and significant personal commitment, all of which are often in short supply. Keep the topic small, focus on baby steps and work towards a win – don't set them up to fail before they start.

> *Coaching questions*
> ◆ How much time will you need to invest in making this happen?
> ◆ Can you spare the time and energy to deliver this?
> ◆ How much leverage will this have on the change you want to make?

Make it measurable

Now you know the client is working on just one change that is under their control and can be delivered in time, you can help them to think about measuring the outcome. Too many coaching changes use vague topics rooted in vague outcomes. If the change and the outcome are vague, the client never knows when they have delivered the outcome and hence the coach can never really know if they've made a difference.

Your skills as a coach will be seen in how you ground the outcome in measurable objectives. These indicate in specific and defined terms the observable results to be attained from the coaching. They are also known as 'outcome objectives'. When applied to coaching support they:

◆ provide a clear and measurable definition of success for both you and the client

◆ enable both coach and client to focus on what is important and to ignore the fluff

◆ enable both client and coach to assess the effectiveness of their work

◆ enable both people to identify what they could do
   differently or better next time round

◆ enable you to establish payback for investment in that
   person.

When helping the client to create a specific
and measurable outcome you need to agree
what needs to be done, within what time
frame and what good and bad will look like.
This concrete outcome needs to be estab-
lished in order to measure the progress while undertaking the
coaching support and at the end. Measuring progress enables
you to keep the client on track to deliver the agreed outcome.

*measuring progress
enables you to keep
the client on track*

Coaching questions

◆ What does the outcome expressly look like?

◆ How will you know if the outcome has been achieved –
   what is the measure of success?

◆ How can we measure progress during the coaching cycle?

Check if it will have real impact

If you've agreed a coaching topic that is subjective, singular,
small and specific then the final question is, so what? What
is the value of this to the client and does it have enough payback to be worthwhile? In short, is it *significant*?

This notion of significance is interesting – namely because
what is significant for one person may be inconsequential for
another. For example, whilst running a coaching programme,

I confessed how I was trying to cut my intake of sweets, how important this was to me and how pleased I was that I didn't buy a pack of wine gums in the garage that morning. A delegate on the course laughed and said it wasn't important. My response to them was that it may not be important to them but to me it would have a profound and lasting impact on my life. I described this by using a choice chain example:

- Not buying the sweets that morning proved I could say no.

- This means that I can say no tomorrow.

- If I can say no for two days then that means I can say no for 100 days.

- At the end of 100 days a new habit will have been created, which is to buy an apple instead of sweets in the garage.

- This means that my calorific intake is reduced dramatically and my vitamin intake increases significantly.

- This means that over a year I would lose about 2 stone.

- This means that I would get down to my recommended BMI weight. (I did, by the way, and lost 7 stone.)

- This means it would help me to live longer.

- This means that I would be better able to support my children while they needed me around.

There was a huge and significant link between that one packet of sweets and how I live the rest of my life and try to be a good parent. The important thing is to identify the correlation between the change in behaviour that the client needs to make today and the significance that will have for the rest of their life. Always question if this significance is enough to help them change and maintain new habits.

You should not judge if the topic is significant but rather help test the significance of the change for the client. Their role is to ensure that the coaching topic is important enough for them to invest the necessary time and energy so that you do not both waste a lot of time, energy and money.

Coaching questions

◆ Why is this change important to you?

◆ How does this coaching topic link to other things or people in your life?

◆ If this is resolved, what value does it offer and is it worth the investment you have to make?

Ready, aim and fire

It is all too easy when working with a client to kick off the coaching without undertaking the necessary preparation. This is akin to trying to aim the gun after it has been fired. By using the five tests described on pages 7–8 you are effectively putting in place a pre-flight check.

Whether you are a new or experienced coach, the notion of a pre-flight check is crucial. If you don't have a basic checklist in place to ensure and assure the client is ready to be coached, you will waste your and their time. I would suggest that the need to formalise the process is also critical – in the same way that a pilot will have a written list of things to check before a flight, so too should a coach, as well as some sort of memory checker to help ensure that the core aspects are covered:

- ◆ Subjective – Is it is about them?

- ◆ Singular – Is it just one thing?

- ◆ Small – Is it manageable?

- ◆ Specific – Is it measurable?

- ◆ Significant – Will it have impact?

These five tests will add immense value to your coaching skills and I guarantee will reap massive rewards for both you and the client in the long run. They will help ensure that you are coaching the right person at the right time and on the right topic.

3

Always work in three dimensions

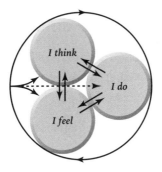

AS A COACH YOU WILL HAVE a relationship with three different clients. The emotional client, who gets excited about things, gets despondent and may alter their mind on an hour by hour or minute by minute basis. The logical client, who makes rational decisions, argues from a sound perspective but can be cursed with limiting thoughts that are manifested as fantasies about their inability to change or be successful.

Finally the physical client, who displays various patterns of behaviour – some of which they are conscious of and others which occur at a tacit level and they are not even aware of.

3D forces

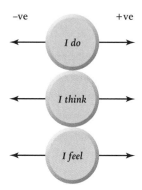

Every choice has three dimensions

We are all made up of a complex system involving the inter-action of action, emotions and thoughts. These three core dimensions are:

◆ the heart – affective or feeling-based factors

◆ the head – cognitive or what people are thinking or saying to themselves

◆ the hand – behavioural or physiological factors (i.e. what people do).

This way of looking at people is not new or unique. It is the basic view that goes back to the Greeks and probably the Egyptians. It views people as composed of three interdependent processes. All parts interact and no one part can change without the other parts also changing. Your role is to understand the client to such an extent that you can help them move each part of themselves in the direction they want to go.

Once you understand the parts, you can challenge the client to see whether each dimension is ready to change. Changing how people 'think' will not deliver performance improvement unless they change what they 'do' and 'feel'. Changing what they 'do' will not be sustainable unless they modify how they 'think' and 'feel'. Changing how they 'feel' will lead to little action unless they change what they 'do' and 'think'. These three simple statements are as fundamental to the art and science of change as Newtonian law is to the rules of thumb used by NASA scientists to land a man on the moon.

Changing one dimension is pointless and will in most cases lead to a reversion back to old ways of behaving. Along with this will be a possible sense of personal failure and a desire to blame someone or something – and in most cases the person blamed will be the coach.

Changing two things may well provide a 'successful' outcome – but I would argue that it is unlikely to be sustainable. Unless the client can use the two forces to fight or resist the other one then reversion is likely

changing one dimension is pointless

to occur. Again the sense of failure and self-blame will be apparent. If the client doesn't understand why the reversion happened they will probably fall into the same trap again.

Once the client learns how to change all three dimensions in relation to their coaching topic, they can begin to exert some control over the forces and how they impact their behaviour. Imagine the person who suffers from a fear of presenting to an audience because they lack confidence in their ability. Becoming emotionally anxious prior to presenting to a large audience might trigger panic thoughts of 'it will all go wrong' – which in turn leads to moist palms and shaky hands. The shaky hands create a thought of 'everyone will see my hands tremble when I put the slide up' – which in turn creates further emotional anxiety. So the ever-decreasing spiral can be seen to bounce between the three dimensions. The person who learns to conquer this fear may do so through a range of strategies. They have dealt with the limiting belief of fantasies played out in their head of 'I am not worthy' and instead replaced it with a voice that said, 'I can only control my presentation – I can't control how the audience responds.' At an emotional level they managed to deal with the deep-seated panic through the use of calming techniques they practised over and over again with the coach. They did this by walking into places where crowds would meet and just talking to strangers. Eventually the fear of new people faded to the background to a point where it became second nature to walk into a room of strange people and just say hello, smile and then begin their pitch.

Dimension forces

For each of these three aspects, certain elements of what a client thinks, feels and does will support their change but other parts will act as a negative force (see figure opposite).

Think about working with someone who is trying to give up smoking and the positive and negative parts of the person that could be present. There might be a positive hand in that the client has been suffering from a really bad chest and

3D trigger and responses

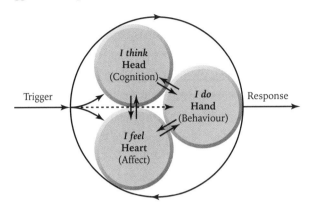

after coughing their lungs up for the third time this week the physical pain might be such that it helps to creative positive energy to say no to a cigarette. But fighting against this will be the fact that they have been smoking since the age of 14 and so the body has a physical dependency or craving for the nicotine. Nicotine is a powerful stimulant that causes us temporarily to feel physically energised. If you have ever smoked you would clearly remember that physical rush that occurs after the first few drags. With the first puff, the heart beats faster, the pulse quickens, veins constrict and blood pressure increases. These are powerful biological forces. So we can see there is a physical battle between these two forces – one that you *cannot* fix, only the client can do this. The coaching aspect is about helping the client to understand what battle has to be fought and then helping them to create a battle plan.

At the logical level the client might know that it is not healthy to smoke. They might appreciate that their partner doesn't want them to smoke and they might not want their child to see them smoking. It appears they can recognise that all logic dictates they should give up now. You might well be exposed to this when the client first asks for help with the change and they explain how it is really important for them to give up and that they are committed to making the change. They might even have worked out how much they can save and ordered a new guitar on the strength of it. But here comes the rub – the logic is fine until they walk into the shop the following morning to get their paper. For the past 25 years they have gone to the local shop to buy a paper, a bar of chocolate for their partner and a packet of cigarettes for themselves. At this point the little voice in their head creates an alternative argument. It suggests that maybe just this one time won't hurt and that as they lasted a whole night without a smoke they deserve a treat. Or the head can create a blank space where they subconsciously choose to forget that they are giving up and then they only remember once the cigarette has been smoked.

help the client develop plans to deal with the dissonant points

This can be described as a logical gap or cognitive dissonance. This is an uncomfortable feeling caused by holding two opposing ideas at the same time. The 'ideas' or 'cognitions' in question may include attitudes and beliefs, and also the awareness of one's behaviour. The mind finds it hard to carry two opposing thoughts at the same time and so will put one of them aside – albeit only temporarily. Hence you must help the client understand that these opposing cognitions will be present for them – potentially for a very long time – and as such develop plans to deal with the dissonant points when they occur.

Finally, for the heart, there can again be two opposing forces that assist or resist the change process. The positive emotional force may be the scare the client had when they noticed their child playing with a sweet and pretending to smoke it like their dad. Or it may come from watching a TV advert that shows how lung decay can occur after many years of smoking. Whatever the trigger, something has happened to promote a powerful emotional force that pushes them to give up smoking. On the other hand, smoking causes the release of natural chemicals in our brain called beta-endorphins. These chemicals cause us to feel more alert and calm. The problem is that nicotine is not stored in the body, so we have to get more and more nicotine to experience these effects. Nicotine alters the levels of certain chemicals in the brain that cause smokers to experience pleasurable changes to mood and concentration. When a smoker stops smoking they crave the nicotine effects and can suffer withdrawal symptoms such as anxiety, depression and irritable moods.

you need to help map these three dimensions

Even before any actions are planned to help the client manage their change, as an absolute you need to help map these three dimensions – in terms of how strong they are, which are the dominant ones and the extent to which they can be turned up or down. By understanding the degree of power in the head, heart and hand elements within the client, you can begin to gauge whether or not the coaching can be successful and, more importantly, can be sustainable. There absolutely will be occasions when you have to say to the client that given the current constraints they may be better off leaving this coaching topic until later as the chances are that it will fail. In the same way that it is stupid to try to paint the outside of a house in a gale force wind, it can be crazy to try to help someone change when you have clear evidence that everything inside the person is screaming out that they are not ready to change.

Using 3D questions

The coaching questions at this stage can be interesting because you are seeking to separate and isolate the three dimensions to understand how they impact on the unwanted behaviour – *and* you need to help the client integrate and pull together the various responses to develop a more systemic or holistic understanding of the choices being made across all three dimensions. When undertaken well this process can be mind-blowing for the client as it is often the point where they understand that coaching is about choices they have to make rather than choices you will make for them.

Coaching questions

- ◆ Hand (I do):
  - – What triggered the behaviour (own, others or object)?
  - – Was it an intentional or instinctive action?
  - – Does the behaviour help achieve the outcome you desire?
  - – What value would alternative behaviours offer?
  - – What other behaviour might help achieve your outcome?
  - – What will help you to create and sustain the behaviour?
  - – How would the new behaviour make you think and feel?

- ◆ Head (I think):
    - – What were you thinking?
    - – What triggered the thought (internal, interaction or innate)?
    - – What value does having this thought have on achieving your outcome?
    - – How intense is the thought?
    - – Could you think of an alternative thought?
    - – What other thoughts might help achieve your outcome?
    - – How would the new thoughts make you feel and behave?

- ◆ Heart (I feel):
    - – What do you feel when the choice is being made?
    - – What triggered the feeling (external or internal)?
    - – Is the feeling pleasant or unpleasant and how intense is it?
    - – What are the consequences of feeling this way?
    - – What alternative feeling would you like at this point?
    - – What value would feeling differently give to you?
    - – How would the new feelings make you think and behave?

- ◆ Integration:
    - – How did/does/will this behaviour make you feel?
    - – What did/does/will this behaviour make you think?
    - – How did/do/will these thoughts make you feel?
    - – How did/do/will these feelings make you behave?
    - – How did/do/will these thoughts make you behave?
    - – How did/do/will these thoughts make you feel?

Working in a 3D world

When you have looked at the client from a 3D perspective then you should be able to:

- define the unwanted behaviour or response that is associated with the coaching topic

- define the emotional or logical trigger that creates this response

- help test the degree of negative strength behind each of these dimensions

- help the client map and measure the positive strength in how they might choose to think, feel and behave to deliver the wanted outcome

- provide support as the client puts together a choice plan that sets out the new choices in how they think, feel and behave and what they need to do to make this choice

- give them support as they try the choices out, review the outcome once tried, amend the choice plan and then repeat where necessary.

Your role is to help the client manage the choice across three dimensions rather than make the choices for them, as so often happens in personal development processes. This is why the vast majority of training, personal development and performance management processes fail; someone else imposes solutions. When you do guide a client towards a solution that truly transforms how they think, feel and behave, you can be assured that the change will be one that sticks.

4

Look at what people *do*, not what they *say*

ONCE A COACHING TOPIC IS AGREED, you've explored the client's motivation and how each part of the client will help serve, not hinder, the goal, the next stage is to ensure that a clear outcome is formed. Part of this is to play devil's advocate and test the goal to ensure that the client has really thought through the purpose of the coaching and what they want to achieve. Clients will often talk about what they want to happen, but then go and behave in ways that are completely counterproductive to this outcome (see figure below). The key here is to ensure that their goal is real and robust, and that what they say and do are completely in sync.

Choice gap

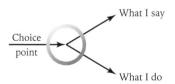

Nathan Myhrvold is a polymath who as a young man did quantum cosmology at Cambridge with Stephen Hawking. He is interesting because of the way he created and delivered his personal goal. He recalled when he was young watching the *Doctor Who* series on the BBC. The Doctor introduces himself to someone who says, 'Doctor? Are you some kind of scientist?' And he says, 'Sir, I am every kind of scientist.' He said that at this point he thought, 'Yes, that is what I want to be: every kind of scientist!' He is now co-founder of Intellectual Ventures, which is seeking to build a large invention portfolio. He personally holds more than 18 US patents and has applied for more than 100.

The point here is that Nathan built a simple goal that gave him immediate direction – he then set off on a journey to deliver this outcome. Look around and think of people you know. Think about the times you have heard them say 'I really want to', 'I am going to' or 'It is important that I'. Now reflect back and consider what percentage of people deliver what they say they are going to. How many people give up smoking and then start again? How many people join the gym and then find that after a few months they have 'more important' things to do? This is the fundamental gap between what people say and what they do – it is this gap that is critical and foundational to the goal of being a successful coach.

how many people give up smoking and then start again?

Understand how people create and build personal goals

This choice gap (between 'say' and 'do') is important for the client because if they fail to deliver what they said they would it can be embarrassing, costly and frustrating. It can create emotional stress as people struggle to deal with some of life's damaging addictions and habits, which they are desperate to erase but find it difficult to resolve. It can also be damaging for you in terms of your professional standing. Like the professional footballer, actor or musician who is only as good as their last performance, each coach is in many ways only as good as their last client's outcomes. If you are coaching people who don't change or who make short-term change and then revert, what does that say about your value in that coaching process? How will the world perceive your ability to help and what damage does this do to your long-term role as a coach?

You should determine a number of factors about the client and their coaching topic:

◆ Are they goal oriented – do they tend to set clear goals as a natural course?

◆ Do they tend to hit their outcomes?

◆ What is their percentage hit rate – as this gives a good indicator as to how they will operate within the coaching partnership?

◆ If they don't hit their goal what reason do they give?

◆ Do they take responsibility for the outcome or do they blame others?

These questions will help to ascertain whether or not there is congruence between what the person says and what they do in life. If there is congruence then the coaching process becomes easier and potentially more successful because you know that what the client says they will do will happen. But if the client has a tendency to say one thing and do another, the energy required to support the person will be greater and also there is an increased chance the outcome will not be successful and probably non-sustainable.

One way to understand the client's 'say/do' habit is to explore how they create and build their personal goals or outcomes. So many people spend their life saying they want to do 'X' – but they end up at 'Y'. This is often because of a lack of clarity or focus on their goal. We often see the following types of goal in play when people make choices.

◆ **Abdicated**: This type of goal is one where a person has decided (consciously or unconsciously) to avoid the problem and give their outcome to someone or something else to manage. Like letting the boss decide what their next job should be or letting a friend tell them if they should get a divorce. In this situation they have given away their goal and avoided the responsibility for making the choice. One of the things to be aware of when dealing with a client with an abdicated goal is that they may well ask you 'what do you think I should do?' – and in effect hand the baton of their life goals to you to look after. First rule, second and last rule of coaching – never take the baton. Once you define the client's goal then all objective value is erased and you take on board responsibility for where they are going.

◆ **Buried**: In this situation someone has a huge desire
   to do something but might be scared, embarrassed
   or prevented from sharing with others what it is they
   want to do. The buried goal can cause real problems
   for both the choice owner and the people around them,
   as it can create difficult situations where people are
   trying to second guess what others want and in the long
   run makes things even worse. In identifying that the
   client has a buried goal they are wary of releasing, you
   will often have to shift from looking at the buried goal
   itself and instead focus on why the client has a fear of
   sharing their goals. Only once this is understood can the
   coaching get back on track and the client be helped to
   formulate a robust outcome.

◆ **Confused**: In this situation someone wants to go to a
   football match, for example, but they also want to spend
   time with their family. Unless they can be creative and
   find a way to accommodate both options then one of
   the choices will take the lead. If they are not clear about
   their real goal then it creates confusion for the other
   people involved in the choice. You need to spend a lot of
   time with this type of client using prioritisation tools to
   help them formulate what is really important and then
   learn to let go (in the short term) of those things that are
   further down the list.

◆ **Directionless**: This is where someone doesn't have
   a goal or doesn't know where they want to go. If they
   don't know where they want to go then how can they
   make a real choice? In effect they are rolling a dice to

manage their life outcomes. This isn't bad as such – but if someone chooses to roll a life dice then they have to accept that their life may well feel out of control and purposeless. Sometimes it is important for the client to understand that an outcome is not a fixed point – it will always be transitory because we have no control over what life will do to us. On this basis it can help the client to pick a goal – irrespective of what it is – just to get something in the firing sights to ensure that mobilisation takes place and the client can learn to value the benefit of a clear goal.

◆ **Espoused**: Here someone says they want to do X and how important it is for them – but when push comes to shove they keep doing Y. Like the person who spends a fortune on diet and fitness programmes only to leave the gym and get a kebab on the way home. In this case the spoken goal is disconnected from the real goal and there is a clear gap between the two. Always look at what people 'do' rather than what they 'say' as this often indicates what their *real* goal is! The real coaching value here comes with being honest with the client and helping them to recognise that the dissonance exists and accept that it doesn't help with managing their life.

◆ **Fixed**: This type of goal is one where people stick with the known and do tomorrow what they did yesterday 'because …' Actually they don't know why they do it – they just always have! And the longer this enduring goal is maintained then the harder it becomes to break. It then becomes one of those accepted rules of life that people don't like to challenge or change. You must beware the emotional outbursts that can occur once the client breaks their rigidity with the past. The risk is that as they seek to break from the old any pent-up emotional anger can be focused on you. Often the challenge with this is to be a sponge and understand that it is not personal – it is just the client letting go.

Always consider asking the client this: '*If you don't know where you want to go – then who does?*' This was so clearly illuminated by Lewis Carroll in the Alice in Wonderland book:

'*One day Alice came to a fork in the road and saw a Cheshire cat in a tree. "Which road do I take?" she asked. "Where do you want to go?" was his response. "I don't know," Alice answered. "Then," said the cat, "it doesn't matter."*'

If your client doesn't know where they want to go or if they are saying one thing and doing another then the whole coaching process will be at risk.

Challenge creates achievable goals

The key outcome for any coaching relationship is to ensure that congruence is created, so that what the person says they will do is what they do and is also aligned with what they will continue to do in the future. You must challenge the client to explore the level of congruence in their life at present and the extent to which they are prepared to deliver on promises made.

You need to question the client to challenge what they say and link that back to what they do. Try to ask about the unspoken issues or maybe challenge the client to produce evidence that backs up any comments they make. As such, the client's attitudes or opinions may well be either reinforced or challenged and their past will be tested to give evidence of action and outcomes. When the dialogue confirms the validity of a person's assertions that there is congruence between what they say and what they do, this adds immense value to both client and coach. It can boost the client's confidence in their ability to deliver their outcomes and it will deliver greater confidence in your faith in the investment in the relationship.

question the client to challenge what they say

You can use a range of questions to challenge the clients say/do focus on the coaching topic. Much can be learned from the idea of appreciative inquiry, where the idea is that people grow in the direction of the questions they are being asked. Every time you ask a question of the client you will influence or move them in a certain direction. If we accept this as a principle then it makes sense for you to ask questions that move the client in directions they may not have considered before. Not in terms of solving the problem for them – rather to ask the questions about their outcome that they have never considered asking themselves. For example, if the client talks about the problems they are having then you may decide to move towards a success orientation and ask outcome questions about how they succeeded in the past, and what they want to accomplish in the future. The appreciative approach of asking what is working and what 'more' would look like will ideally help the client move to a place that is more congruent with the potential goal that lies untapped in the head or heart. When working with clients your goal must be to become clear on what a successful outcome would be and then explore what resources the client may need to achieve it.

Coaching questions

The goal formation questions below aim to strike a difficult balance – to challenge the client about the extent to which their say/do actions are aligned and to help them consider 'what could be' if they gave themselves permission to be more than they dare dream.

◆ **Abdicated:**
  - Where does the coaching goal come from – is it something you decided or was it suggested to you? What would a great goal look like?
  - Do you take responsibility for this goal – are you prepared to accept the gains of the outcome as well as any potential pains of the gain?

◆ **Buried:**
  - If you could paint a picture of the dream you haven't dared to share with anyone, what would it look like? What film reminds you of your deep goal?
  - How would you describe your secret goal to a child?

◆ **Confused:**
  - If you think about your coaching outcome, is there a different outcome that is also important but would clash with this? Which is more important at this moment in time?
  - Is there a third potential outcome – one that will build on both outcomes and that you hadn't thought of before?

◆ **Directionless**:
  – If you don't have a goal at the moment, would you see
    that as a goal in its own right – to choose to roll the
    dice – much like an adventure holiday?
  – If that is the case – with the dice as your goal – how
    do you feel about that? Does it feel OK or would
    you sooner move to a place where you have a more
    defined goal?

◆ **Espoused**:
  – Is there any gap between what you say you want to do
    and what you actually do? If so, why is that?
  – Of the two (what you say and what you do), which
    (if honest with yourself) is the one you really want to
    aim for?

◆ **Fixed**:
  – If we consider your coaching topic, has it changed
    much in recent years? If it has remained unchanged,
    are you happy with that?
  – If you could wave a magic wand would you like to
    create a completely new outcome for yourself and, if
    so, what would that be?

Always align words with deeds

It is not for you to create, find, discover or build the client's goal. That is for the client to undertake – although
you can use questions to help them do this with the least
pain and with minimum fuss. I often hear coaches say they
are going to 'light a fire' under their client – but in all hon-
estly when you try to light fires under people all you get is
a deep smell of burning and a few tears rather than success
that is sustainable.

Your aim should be to help people release and unleash their goal from within. Once this spark has been uncovered then your role is to help fan the flames and enable the fire to stay bright and alight. One of the most significant ways to help fan the flames is by helping the client to ensure that there is congruence between what they say and what they do (see figure below).

help people release and unleash their goal from within

Choice alignment

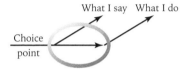

Just imagine if you are driving down a small country road and in one ear your partner is telling you where to go and in the other your parents are shouting at you from the back seat to slow down. How easy is it to drive and get to your end destination? This analogy holds true for coaching – the coach's role is to help turn down the dissenting or confusing voices that cause people to go off track and then turn up the one directional voice that gives a unitary outcome, so that all the energy can be focused on getting to that one place.

Your value as a coach will be in the questions you ask. Coaching is all about challenging the client – it may be difficult (for you and the client), but I guarantee the more you test your client, the more successful the outcome is likely to be.

5

Ask the killer question – 'So what is stopping you?'

FEAR as a reality

Fantasy
Experienced
As a
Reality!

THE MOST EFFECTIVE QUESTION you can ask as a coach is, 'So what is stopping you?' This is because most people 'don't' because they think they 'can't'. The 'can't' is down to deeply embedded limiting beliefs that create a fear of operating in areas that are unknown. Your aim as a coach is to help the client remove their own blockages – how they are stopping themselves from being successful.

Try to understand the client's fears

Your prime goal is to help the client to see their world in a new way. This isn't about seeing it your way – just from a different viewpoint. In doing this they can see the problem in a new light and then see how they can resolve the issue. By doing this you are not fixing the problem – you are just holding up a mirror for them to look at themselves from a different perspective.

help the client to see their world in a new way

To achieve this the client has to be prepared to discard or throw away their current world view and accept an alternative frame of reference. In making this shift, a self-sustaining loop must be broken. This loop is a common process; people see the world in a particular way and so expect it to behave according to the criteria set out in their own particular mental map. For example, the client might say, 'I have a tendency to be late for meetings.' They therefore accept that being late is part of who they are and that they will always be late for meetings. It is this lock into failure language that causes the client to hold on to a personal failure model.

For a client to change, you must help them break the current pattern of behaviour and support a shift to a new way of thinking (see figure opposite).

The trick is for you to help the client identify any limiting boundaries they currently operate within and then understand how to stretch these boundaries. We all have personal limitations that are imposed by us, by external factors, or jointly. These are the maps that we operate to.

Changing the client's mind

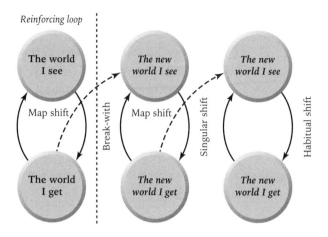

Fear is often a fantasy and not a fact

Our mental maps become distorted over time and what appears to be the truth to the client can seem at odds to the coach. Often clients seem perfectly happy in what may appear to be performance-limiting activities – to them they are normal and OK. Your role is to listen carefully to the client as they describe their problem and understand the extent to which the problem is routed in a distorted or limited view of themselves. Once you can see the distortion and how it is impacting their coaching topic then you might also be able to understand what caused the distortion or fantasy to occur. Examples of coaching topics and the source of distortion are shown in the table overleaf.

Coaching topic	Example source of distortion
Lack of self-confidence	Possibly brought up by parents who failed to help the client have sense of self-belief
Overeating	Might be where sugar and sweets were given by parents as a reward when young
Fear of presenting	School presentation where the client was ridiculed by the teacher in front of classmates
Want to sing but no ability	Told by friends *at a young age that their voice is no good*
Unwilling to take life risks	Family values that have safety and security as the prime goals

This distortion can be almost imperceptible and driven by many factors, including personal values, political forces, fears or simple forgetfulness. The shift from hard, objective data to subjective fiction can quite rapidly take the client through a number of stages:

◆ I see something happen that is quite factual.

◆ I select details from what I observe, based on my beliefs and values.

◆ I use these details and add my personal meanings, based on personal experiences.

◆ This view shifts from interpretation to hard fact.

◆ I take actions and change my behaviour, based on these new beliefs.

A fantasy ladder, as shown in figure opposite, can be used to illustrate this process.

Fantasy ladder

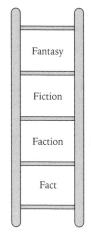

Now has little relation to the original fact and has turned into myth or story.

The story has its roots in fact, but critical details have been modified.

One person has put a spin on it, so it's still basically true, but it now has a personalised edge.

All people invloved in the experience would agree the details.

At the bottom of the ladder is a fact or event that has happened to the client. They select elements of the event and turn it into *faction*, something that is basically true but is influenced and modified by their map of the world. The faction turns into fiction, as the biased story is translated into a distorted view of what happened – although some elements of the fact can be found, you would have to dig quite deep to uncover the real events. Finally, the fiction turns into fantasy as the story takes on mythical status (but is real to the client). This may be triggered by the original fact but has nothing to do with it in terms of either content or detail.

A real example can be found with someone I know who loved swimming, so much so that they deliberately purchased a property with a swimming pool. But whilst they were happy to swim during the day, they refused to swim at night. After a degree of pushing and challenging it turned out that they had a powerful fear that there would be a shark in there! Although this might seem crazy to an outsider, to them (even though the rational part of them knew this to be false) once darkness came there was a real and possible chance that a shark would be at the bottom. After digging deeper I discovered that this fantasy came from seeing the film *Jaws* as a child, which had left a lasting impact.

Beware when the client's fear becomes a 'fact'

So a FEAR pattern might simply be described as a fantasy that someone experiences as a reality. At the time of impact it is completely real and absolute for them. Before or after the event they may well understand that the fantasy is untrue – but at the point of impact it is true for them (see figure opposite).

Until the client is helped to climb down the ladder and operate at a fact level, the coaching process will have very little chance of sustainable success.

Learn to identify FEAR patterns

The climb up the fantasy ladder doesn't have to involve other people. This is something that a client will do individually, and often in seconds. Think about the last time you made a presentation to an audience. All's going well until you realise that the man at the end of the third row is not paying attention. As you look closer you realise that he is actually typing on his laptop. Immediately the insecurity driver kicks in, and you think that your presentation is failing. You start to climb

Fantasy as a FEAR

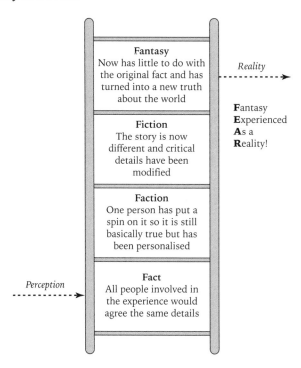

up to the faction level as you conclude that other people are probably not interested either and are just looking interested to be polite. Then you reach the fiction stage, where you believe that your presentational style is all wrong. You're not clever enough, you look a mess and you don't have any funny stories to draw upon like the really good presenters. By the end, you've made a headlong jump into fantasy and decided that you'll never do any more of this type of presentation – you're not up to it and it's far better coming from someone who knows what they are doing.

This leap up the fantasy ladder is a common event and one that people beat themselves up over on a daily basis. If not during a presentation then it might be how people react in a team meeting, at a family gathering or at college. The point is that we often climb the fantasy ladder without any real need to. We let the distorted drivers build conclusions about us and others that are unclear or totally false. In the case of the presentation, it might have been that the man at the end of the row was really enthused about the session

we often climb the fantasy ladder without any real need to

and wanted to capture all the elements that weren't in the overheads. Unless you can help the client to climb down the ladder and operate at fact level, they will be forever operating in fantasy land.

As we see clients go up and down the fantasy ladder, it becomes possible to highlight a series of different FEAR patterns. These patterns, outlined below, are the internal personal routines that typically block the coaching process from working.

◆ **Absotruths** – making sweeping conclusions about a minor situation and turning it into an absolute truth. This can include creating false labels for oneself and others – for example, 'because I didn't pass the interview I am crap and will never get a new job'. Or, 'because the person didn't acknowledge my hello in the corridor that means they don't like me'.

◆ **Be the best** – setting targets that are far beyond the plausible levels that can be met by most people. This is referred to as 'musturbation' as it highlights the way people use unconditional shoulds and musts – in the belief that things must happen for them to be 'good'. They must be loved, they should achieve certain goals and they must do well in all things.

- **Choice capping** – only seeing two options when there are many possible actions that can be taken. This can be seen at the solution stage of a coaching session, when the client swears blind that they only have two possible solutions and really believe that there are no other options available.

- **Discounting the positives** – choosing to turn down the positives and turn up the negatives. In many cases people will absolutely refuse to listen to positive feedback even when it is thrust in their face.

- **Emotional overload** – letting emotions rule what seems to be a logical choice and the person believing they are being rational – so the heart tricks the head into believing that it makes sense!

- **Faking it** – believing that one day the truth will out and people will discover that you're really no good. Common when people are rapidly promoted within an organisation and are not convinced that it is warranted.

- **Guessing game** – believing that you can see into the unknown. This might be an ability to look into the future and predict what will happen or to look into other people's minds and know what they are thinking.

Always have the courage to challenge the FEAR patterns

The fantasy ladder can help to identify why people think the way they do and behave in ways that don't sometimes appear to make sense. In most cases clients don't know why they do what they do – it is just the way that they have always operated. Their thoughts, feelings and behaviours have been pushed into a deep memory that is long forgotten, and in many cases people would sooner not remember why. I see this in the beliefs that are instinctually passed on to children – 'You should buy your own home', 'It is wrong to lie' or 'Be careful who you trust'. These are in effect fantasies about life passed on to children as facts. If they ask why then we might struggle to give a robust answer – it is just something that is seen as a personal truth.

clients don't know why they do what they do

Your aim is to help the client get to a position where they can discard those fantasies that are blocking their ability to move forward. Although the client cannot live their life without either creating distorted beliefs or picking up fantasies from other people, you can help them move to a position where they can choose to discard those that limit their ability to change. You can do this by:

◆ helping the client to become more conscious of their thinking and feeling patterns through a process of internalisation and contemplation

◆ helping the client make this reflection more visible to themselves by verbalising how they think and feel

◆ using this deeper understanding to explore how other people make sense of the world, and through this creating a more informed view of the choices they want to make.

To help the client develop this pattern of internalisation, vocalisation and investigation you can draw upon a range of simple challenges and questions. Once the client voices a specific fantasy (for example, 'I can't present to a group', 'I am shy' or 'I don't have any skills'), you can use any one of the following routines to challenge the statement.

◆ **Ask the audience** – You can ask the client, 'Would other people support the view or is it just your view?' The point with this is to encourage the client to step outside their frame of reference and look at themselves from an external perspective.

◆ **Taste test** – Encourage the client to work from the facts back rather than the belief forward. Encourage them to shift from phrases like 'I think' or 'I know', which are subjective perceptions of a situation, and get them to focus on the facts. Always ask what actually happens, where is the data and what evidence they have.

◆ **Shades of grey** – Try to open out and explore the belief variations: is this always/often/sometimes true? Clients will offer different ranges of truisms that sit on the subjective to objective continuum. For example, this might be 'I can't sing', 'I am not a great singer', 'There are some songs I can't handle', or 'I would like to sing but have never really tried'. If you can help the client to accept that this line exists then this is the first step towards helping them to move to a more objective view of their situation.

◆ **Phone a friend** – Ask what advice they would give to a friend who said these things. Invoking the idea of a friend can help the client to step into another person's map of the world.

◆ **Redefine** – Ask what this word or statement means – how would they define it? When a client says 'I can't', challenge them to say what this actually means. Encourage them to redefine it and use another term, maybe give them a dictionary to look the word up and explore what it means or use a thesaurus and ask them to find alternative words. This can be very powerful because what clients instinctively say offers a window into their mental models. By asking them to look in that window to see it from the outside in can help them to step back and reframe beliefs that were entrenched. Helping a client to move from 'I can't' to 'Can I?' is one of the most powerful coaching outcomes that can be delivered. One of the slickest tricks a dodgy salesperson can play on a punter is to subliminally shift their language patterns and so create a subconscious buying pattern. In the same way the mind can play tricks, and by the use of negative language (I can't, I don't, or it isn't me) we begin to believe what we hear ourselves say. A key part of your role is to unpick these lazy patterns and help the client reprogram themselves.

◆ **Relabel** – Often when faced with a coaching challenge the client will frame their topic in an emotional wrapper – which can both distort and amplify its meaning. The question is, can the client use less emotional language and be more logical in the way they present their issue? By stripping the emotion from the statement it allows you and the client to be more clinical in your analysis of the situation.

- ◆ **What if?** – Ask what if this were true – what would that mean (positives and negatives)? This takes a different approach – and rather than challenge the client to let go of the statement, you can ask what if it were true – what would that mean? By forcing the client to deal with and confront the consequences of their statement it seeks to turn a potentially abstract and vague fantasy into a fact. By asking 'what if?', the client is forced to explore the meaning of what they are projecting to the world. The upside with this is that it can confront and bring to the surface a sense of reality quite rapidly; the downside is that is can be like watching a slow motion car crash – as the client is willing to embrace the fantasy as a fact and then wallow in it. This is a real risk you will need to watch for.

The whole point of these routines is not to follow them slavishly – rather they are examples of a genre of ideas that are designed to help the client climb down from the fantasy ladder. The essence of the idea behind the fantasy ladder is that coaching doesn't have to be onerous, doesn't have to take months and doesn't have to end in tears. What it can do is help change someone's life by the use of a few simple questions.

Using questions to fight the fear

This stage can be difficult for both you and the client because of the need to challenge on three levels:

◆ What they feel

◆ What they think

◆ What they do.

Only by helping the client to be really honest about what they feel, think and do can you help move them forward. This is why the questions you ask are so critical and can have such a huge impact on the final outcome.

Coaching questions

◆ Turn down the volume:
  - Is this always the case – are there times when this doesn't happen?
  - Are there times when things work well?
  - What do you mean when you say things like always, every time or never?
  - What would you say if you heard someone else say something like that?

◆ Clean the distortion:
  - What makes you think this is true?
  - Who told you that was the case?
  - What would have to happen for you to change your mind on this?
  - What if this were not true?

◆ Add more data:
- Can you describe the incident in more detail?
- What were you thinking and feeling at the time?
- What were you doing and how did other people respond to that?
- How would other people who were there describe what happened?

In many if not most cases the client will fight your challenge

These types of question prompt a line of thinking which moves people from a perception that they have no choice to realising that they do in fact have choice and possibilities for change. But it is entirely normal for people to resist if they feel that someone is challenging their sense of reality and what is 'right' for them.

A typical exchange might go like this:

Client: 'I cannot talk to my boss about my problems.'

Coach: 'What would happen if you did?'

Client: 'I would feel very awkward.'

Coach: 'So I guess you could talk to your boss about difficult issues but you would simply feel embarrassed doing so.'

Client: 'Yes, I suppose I could.'

Coach: 'So what choice could you make to help achieve your goal?'

This type of coaching challenge is very quick and relatively easy for both coach and client. The power is that once the client understands and accepts that there are other ways of looking at their coaching topic then there is a greater chance that they will accept there are other choices that can be made. In doing this the fantasy belief has been disrupted and potentially eradicated. This opens the option for you to help the client to look at new choices and explore the value of different ways of looking at their situation. The key to this process is to help the client climb down the fantasy ladder and see their world map in a new way.

You can help the client shift from fantasy to fact

Your aim is to minimise and reduce the impact that the distortion process has had in corrupting the client's view of themselves and others. As seen in figure below, the aim is to help the client climb down the ladder.

Climbing down the fantasy ladder

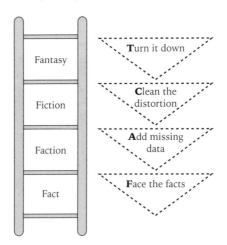

The four key questioning activities used to counteract the processes can be seen in the table below. This is the 'FACT' model and follows this pattern:

Counter force	Question description
Turn it down	Turn down the volume that the client hears in their head. Help erase statements like 'I always' or 'I never' as these are generalisations that blind them to other ways of looking at the world. Typical questions might be, 'Will it always be the case?' and 'Do you believe that you will never be able to?'
Clean the distortion	Once the generalisation has been cleared, you will seek to counteract the distortion that the client has embedded in their world map. They will want to ask, 'What makes you think that this is true?' or 'How do you know this?' It is at this stage that you will tend to fight back with responses such as 'I know it' or 'I have been told', as this is the point where you will be directly challenging the client's deep belief systems – beliefs that are so entrenched they are often not aware of them at a conscious level.
Add missing data	Once understood, encourage them to include other data from that same event and help them to take a wider and more objective view of the situation. Ask, 'What did other people say?', 'What else did you do?' or 'Why do you think they said that?' The aim is to try to turn down the data that corrupted their view and turn up other perspectives. So if a child is told by a parent that 'the green dress doesn't suit them', maybe ask them what other people said, or what they thought about it or what other people look like in green. Limit the impact of the corrupting statement and encourage a broader view.
Face the facts	Once you have helped to turn down the force of the limiting belief, challenged why it was there in the first place and then encouraged a broader and richer view of the situation – this can help to open out the client's viewpoint so that they can take a much more reasoned view of their situation. You have now helped the client to face the fact and see to what extent their perception of a situation is correct or incorrect.

What the client sees is what they get

In most cases you will always find that clients are sabotaging themselves in one way or another with FEAR patterns. The more you can help the client prevent these beliefs from getting in the way of their real potential, the greater value you will add to the client. In working with the FEAR patterns, remember that:

◆ the FEAR patterns are fantasy and not necessarily a fact – so they can be changed

◆ most of them take time to change – so stick with it

◆ some of the FEAR patterns are based upon very deep and instinctive patterns that come from deep emotional responses – in this case you might not change them but you can help the client to find ways to deal with them.

If your client is basing their goal on FEAR patterns from the past then they will always underestimate what they might be able to achieve – so before seeking to create a positive outcome ensure that the FEAR patterns are put to bed. Remember, in most cases, what people see is what they get. You might not be able to change how they behave, but you can help them to see the world in a different way – and that can create new behaviours, new dreams and new ways of behaving.

6

Learn to push the pause button

ALL GREAT COACHING is about changing how people think, feel and behave. To help this happen, the client needs to become more self-aware – more aware of these three factors.

Just like a video – you can press the pause button to see the detail

A pause/play point (PPP) is used to understand and explore how a particular thought, feeling or behaviour impacts on a coaching topic. The PPP can be identified or targeted in various ways, but typically clients are asked to tell a story about a recent experience they have had that is related (directly or indirectly) to their coaching topic. A PPP might be:

◆ one specific aspect of their work that went particularly well and they want to understand why

◆ a piece of work that they found really hard and that ended up causing stress

♦ a certain time when they behaved in a way to a colleague that they felt was inappropriate

♦ an incident where they maybe didn't follow a diet or fitness regime that they had set out to follow.

the PPP is a simple but amazingly powerful tool

The PPP is a simple but amazingly powerful tool that allows you rapidly to get to the core of the problem, the root cause and its potential resolution. It is underpinned by five key steps:

1 Identify the PPP that the client wishes to talk about.

2 Ask the client to tell their story so that the facts can be gathered.

3 Once the facts (and not the fantasies) are gathered, seek to drill down and get to the nub of the problem (which in many cases is not the one the client believed it to be).

4 Agree with the client what root issues or themes emerge from the discussion about the key incident.

5 Agree what the primary aspects of the PPP are that need to be addressed to help deal with the coaching topic.

The great thing about this way of working is that it is very flexible and not locked into a particular methodology or systemic approach. It is a conversational process that can be carried out in a clinical setting, in a coffee shop or in the back of a cab. In addition, the information is collected from the client using their words and so offers a lot of subtle clues, as you see not just what the client describes but also how they describe it and what emotions they display. Because it starts with a story as opposed to a problem it can help to identify issues that both client and coach may have missed in other conversations – like watching a film and suddenly realising that the real baddie is not the one that was suspected all along. Finally, it transfers ownership firmly to the client to take a key and dominant role in the diagnostic part of the journey. It is not about you identifying a problem – rather the client peels back the onion to discover what is at the core of the coaching topic, and as such they adopt a far higher level of ownership of the outcome.

The first problem that can occur with the PPP approach is that because the event is offered up by the client it can be open to bias and misinterpretation by them. This might be an overt misreporting as they seek to avoid the truth because of fear or embarrassment about the topic. Or it might be a case that their memory has played tricks on them and they have internally reinterpreted those things that happened. So the story may be imprecise and widely off beam from what really happened. Second, the method can have an implicit bias towards stories that happened recently as these are more open to instant recall. This is not to say that these have less value – but sometimes you may need to encourage the client to step back in time and seek to recall incidents that occurred over a longer time period. Finally, some clients may see the simple telling of a story that is not directly linked to the coaching topic as immaterial or a waste of time. So you must pay careful attention to explaining why the broader appreciation of how they have behaved in different contexts can have a profound impact on the coaching topic.

encourage the client to step back in time

Use the pause point as if it were a camera lens

The first thing you need to do to help the client push the pause button is help them step back from a specific incident and see it from a wider plane. When people are struggling with a problem they tend to focus on just this and can be blinded to how it fits with the real world. Try to help them step back, turn down the intensity and instead take a broader look at what has happened. Once the client can see the item to be considered in a more grounded way, you can use the five-point pause model shown below to pull out the story in more detail.

Pause point stages

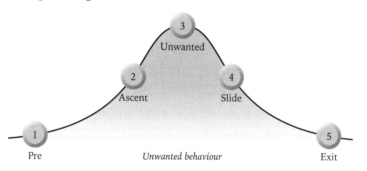

You can use a timeline to do this. As the client's story unfolds, break the time sequence down into five distinct stages:

1 **Pre** – the things that happened prior to the unwanted behaviour.

2 **Ascent** – the first steps that moved the client into the unwanted territory.

3 **Unwanted** – in specific terms the thing that happened.

4 **Slide** – exiting the peak and moving out of the unwanted area.

5 **Exit** – the point at which regret, embarrassment or frustration sets in, typically when the client wishes they could rewind the clock.

For example, if you are coaching someone who has a weight problem, you might ask the client to talk about the last time they behaved in a way that they later regretted. They might talk about how they walked down the high street thinking about what soap powder they needed to pick up (point 1 – Pre stage). As they approach a baker's and smell the rich aromas coming out of the door they suddenly picture a doughnut and their mouth begins to water. At this point they have shifted to point 2 on the model (Ascent). Finally, it happens – they turn right, enter the shop and buy a rich jam-filled doughnut. Now they are at point 3 on the timeline, thoroughly enjoying the food without a care in the world. At stage 4 they might experience a mix of thoughts and feelings. There might be satisfaction because of the sensory pleasure the doughnut gave them but a few doubting questions may also enter their head. This has moved them towards stage 5. Now at point 5 (Exit) they might begin to regret what has happened and curse themselves for walking down the high street when they knew there would be temptations along every step.

Your role here is to encourage them to reflect on what happened and chart the change they experienced over a set time frame. Once the pause point is mapped (although the client may feel uncomfortable), you should encourage the client to repeat the story – as many times as is necessary to really pull out every nuance of what they were thinking, feeling and doing at each of the five points on the timeline. You are looking to help the client identify the point at which the first trigger occurred. The aim is to show the client that, in most cases, the failure point does not happen at the point of unwanted action, but much earlier. With the example above, it's not when the doughnut is being eaten, but is perhaps the choice to walk down a specific street or deciding not to eat breakfast that morning. It is about understanding that there is a sequence of patterns and choice points that led to the unwanted behaviour. By charting these you can help the client determine the trigger point and avoid it next time.

If the client has deeply embedded habits, it is important not to be too ambitious. The trick is to agree a game plan that the client can win – don't set them up for a failure. Hence the coaching might not be about shutting down the behaviour completely, it may just be a case of helping the client to manage the various pause points. Eventually they should get to the stage where they can push the pause button at stage 1 and so avoid those later stages (see figure opposite).

agree a game plan that the client can win

No matter what the coaching topic, whether the client is trying to change a bad habit into a good one, the pause button will be of immense value. The key thing is for the client to appreciate that they do have a choice – they can choose their responses and it is never too late to change these.

Pushing the pause button

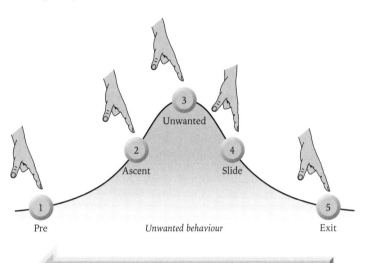

Coach helps client to move pause point back along the timeline

Coaching questions

In helping the client to push the pause button, there is a simple pattern of questioning you can follow that will help them make sense of the pause process and also learn to push the button for themselves.

◆ What is the choice you wish to change?

◆ Why do you want to change it?

◆ What benefit would you get from a new choice?

◆ Can you see the five pause stages that surround the choice being made?

◆ How long does it take you to go through them?

◆ What happens in the lead-up to the unwanted choice?

◆ How do you feel after and what do you say to yourself?

◆ Do you think you might be able to push the pause button before it happens next time?

◆ At what point might you realistically be able to push the pause button next time?

◆ What can I do to help you push the button?

◆ What can you do now to help yourself push the pause button next time?

◆ What triggered the behaviour (own, others or object)?

◆ Was it an intentional or instinctive action?

◆ Does the behaviour help achieve the outcome you desire?

◆ How does it make you feel?

◆ What does it make you think?

◆ What other behaviour might help achieve your outcome?

◆ What will help you to create and sustain the behaviour?

◆ How would the new behaviour make you think and feel?

When using these questions, try to draw the pause diagram shown on page 64 and ask the client to trace their journey; actually seeing the route to success makes a huge difference.

7

If the client doesn't know what good looks like, how will they know when they are there?

CLIENTS OFTEN TALK ABOUT their dreams and goals in a way that sounds amazing and inspirational. But when you start to unpick the detail it becomes clear that they haven't really thought it through properly, they don't understand what impact it will have on their current life and, in reality, they are unlikely to enjoy it if they achieve it! It's essential that the reality of the achieved goal is understood and that you are both working towards something your client actually wants. Help them to reach out and touch the outcome.

a well-formed coaching outcome is more than just a goal

You need to help your client develop a well-formed outcome. In many ways a well-formed coaching outcome is more than just a goal. It is about helping the client to create a positive outcome that they want to hit and helping them test the richness – the appeal – of the goal. The result is, ideally, not a goal that can be written on a piece of paper or in a diary, it is about the ownership of something that is real, tangible and a part of the client's daily passion and purpose. The major benefit of doing this is that the client ends up moving towards an outcome without realising the changes they are making in their life.

As you use outcome-based coaching, you will give the client confidence that the goal is under their control to deliver. They should be able to taste the final stage and be willing to bet on themselves to achieve it. If they enter the coaching cycle with any real uncertainty about their ability to reach the goal then question whether they are ready to start the journey.

Also, outcome-based goals help to move the goal from a vague statement to a richer and more sensory-based description. If someone said they wanted a 'good life' then that is interesting but tells us little. But if they describe how life will be once they have it, what they will give up to get it and how they will measure that achievement, the goal becomes real – you can see it and, therefore, achieve it.

Use of this approach has a valuable impact on setting a clear goal and identifying when deviation occurs. It's an extremely useful tool, therefore, to evaluate progress – to see when things are going off track, because of the client *or* the coach. For both parties, there can be a risk of either avoiding the difficult areas or getting overenthusiastic and generating scope creep in the journey.

How to test whether an outcome is wanted and achievable

Your role is to act as an investigator and catalyst, to help draw out a realistic, tangible and measurable solution for the client, consumer and consultancy team. You can help achieve this by asking seven simple questions in the OUTCOME framework (see below).

your role is to act as an investigator and catalyst

Testing the outcome

● ● ● Ownership
● ● ● Unease/urge
● ● ● Trade-off
● ● ● Changed
● ● ● Others
● ● ● Measure
● ● ● Engage

◆ **Owns**: Who owns the outcome and is it self-maintained? Are they ready, able and willing to make this happen or are they trying to change something outside their field of control? Ultimately, at the end of the coaching partnership, you will move on and the client will be expected to maintain the change. The question is, do they have the desire and capability to hold the gains or will other external forces erode any movement forward?

◆ **Unease/urge**: What triggered the need for change? Ask why the coaching topic is really important at a deep, rather than superficial, level. Why has the issue surfaced now and what priority does it hold over other issues?

This can take two forms. The first might be a 'running from' statement – where they see a problem that they want to eradicate. The other option is a 'running to' description – which is a future-oriented goal that they wish to achieve and is not linked to dissatisfaction with now. Neither is right or wrong – we need to understand and ensure that clients understand their motivational driver. Some clients will seek to describe a 'running to' coaching topic that is in reality a 'running from'. This can be dangerous as there will often be a temptation on their part to take the first good thing that comes along without really understanding the consequences of that choice. In most cases this delivers short-term success but is non-sustainable, and they revert to the old ways and habits within a relatively short period of time.

- **Trade-off**: This is the real test of how important the topic is for the client to achieve. You need to ask what will have to be given up to achieve the change. It is often forgotten that people adopt certain practices or behaviours because there is a payback. Achieving a goal means that something will be gained and something will be lost. The client must think through and appreciate the potential loss before they can confirm what outcome is required.

- **Changed**: This is the sensory question, typically based around how life will be different when the change is made. At this point the client has clarified the desired outcome and you can help to solidify the changes. One way of doing this is by asking the client to take a mental step forward in time – to consider how life will be different at the end of the project. They are asked to move into the future and imagine what life will be like. You have to help them move into the future at this point and do anything that helps them actually 'be' there. Key questions are, when the outcome is achieved what will they be feeling, thinking and doing? It is this movement along the timeline into a new space that is important – both to help test if the outcome is for them and to test if they are serious about making the change.

◆ **Others**: It is very rare that a client will seek to make a change that doesn't impact on other people in their life. If it doesn't, one might even ask what the point is! However, you must help the client to test how the change will impact others and what their response is likely to be. Ask what impact the change will have on colleagues, friends and family – will there be losers and winners as a consequence of the action they are taking? In effecting a change, one of the dangers is that short-term and urgent forces are responded to and little attention is paid to the impact that the change will have on other parties or groups. From this the client should be able to offer a realistic picture of who will be affected by the proposed change and, more importantly, what reaction can be anticipated. Will there be people who seek to block the actions they plan to take and are their key stakeholders who will be able to help them on the journey? At the end of the stage the client should be able to explicitly identify the blockers and backers and what action they might need to take with each group to ensure they achieve the goal.

◆ **Measure**: The important question is often, how will they know when they get there? This is the one that forces the client to turn the vague and abstract goal into something that is tangible and can be measured. Ask the client how they will know if the change has been successful and also what measures can be used along the way to ensure that they don't go off track. To be sure that the outcome is one that the client really wants and can be achieved, they should be able to describe in simple terms how they will 'know' that a successful change has been delivered. Many clients will find this hard and you may well have to offer guidance and support in the formation of tangible criteria.

◆ **Engage**: What value will my role as a coach bring to this relationship? Push the client to describe what they want from you, how they will measure your support, what good coaching looks like and so on. Unless they are clear on the engagement model they are after then the risk is that the partnership will drift into a one-sided game – where you are in control and the client is the subordinate partner. This is not satisfactory and will lead to high dependency setting in and the formation of a solution that is ultimately non-sustainable.

Once you have taken them through the OUTCOME structure, it makes sense to think in more depth and detail about the formation of an action plan. Moving to an action state without the OUTCOME model being completed will lead to problems in the later stages and a lot of wasted time.

Coaching questions

These questions provide a starter for the type of thing you
can ask – but often you have to go with the flow as the
questions will be very driven by the responses that you get
from the client.

◆ Owns:
  – Is this topic under your control?
  – Can anyone prevent you from taking the action?
  – Can you sustain the goal once complete?

◆ Unease/urge:
  – What is the problem you want to address – if the
    problem went would you still need coaching?
  – What is the dream you want to achieve – if you had
    the dream now would you still want coaching?
  – Do you think you are 'running from' or 'running to'
    with this topic?

◆ Trade-off:
  – What energy and effort will this goal need?
  – What is good about the present situation? What do
    you want to keep? What will you have to give up to
    achieve the goal?
  – Which is more important at this moment in time –
    the thing you are losing or what you want to gain?

◆ Changed:
  – When the goal is complete how will life be different?
  – What will you be feeling, thinking and doing
    differently?
  – How will your environment be different – what will
    you see around you?

◆ Measures:
  – What is the current measure of dissatisfaction?
  – How will you measure when the goal is achieved?
  – How will you know on the journey if you are on or off track?

◆ Engage:
  – What value can I offer?
  – What does good coaching support look like and what does bad coaching support look like?
  – What is the one thing that I can do to help you be successful?

The OUTCOME approach will help you to focus the client on what they really want and ensure that it is the optimum outcome for them. This is key because our personal outcomes act as a force to propel us forward – if our outcomes are unclear, vague or misdirected then our journey will, in most cases, lead nowhere.

8

There is only one coaching style – the one that works best for the client

YOUR COACHING STYLE AND APPROACH need to work with the client – not the other way round. To help you find the best approach for your client, the two most important questions to ask are how much structure they will need and how visible they want the coaching process to be (see figure overleaf). Structure means the extent to which you put in place planning and control systems to enable the change to happen. At one end of the spectrum will be the active use of project plans, action plans and systems designed to manage the flow of activities. At the other end of the spectrum you adopt a style that is much more relaxed in nature and is less reliant on the use of formal planning techniques. Visibility is about how noticeable the coaching process is to the coach, client and other people. At one end of this spectrum we have a coaching style that is very visible and overt. The reviews and meetings are more likely to be open. In a work situation they might be held in more formal settings, diaries and be subject to a schedule. At the other end of this spectrum the visibility is very low key, with meetings and reviews taking place on a casual, less diarised basis – perhaps in a coffee shop.

Coaching style options

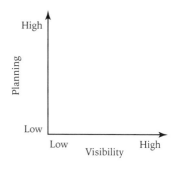

Map the preferred style

As you understand the client's needs in terms of the level of structure and visibility, you will be able to find a coaching style that will work for them. In considering these two drivers, it is possible to identify four loose coaching styles: accidental, backstage, control and debate.

◆ **Accidental**. You help the client develop a clear understanding of where they want to go but not a clear process of how to get there.

◆ **Backstage**. With this approach you develop a clear plan for the coaching process – but the action takes place in the background. The backstage model is one that we use more than we realise – persuading the children to eat their cabbage, hiding a pill in the dog's food or flirting with the boss's PA to get some time in the diary.

◆ **Control**. This follows a planned and visible structure of change, which means making the assumption that you can predict and control your future according to a set of rules.

◆ **Debate**. With a low visibility and low planning approach the coaching is underpinned by a high level of conversation and dialogue.

These four styles can be developed into a simple coaching matrix (see figure below). Each of the four quadrants has a particular coaching style which can be applied in different circumstances.

Coaching styles

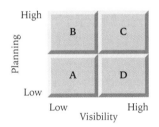

Accidental style – be loose and relaxed

Accidental coaching can be a high-risk strategy and is reliant on the level of trust that you have developed with the client. Your role is to develop a suitable environment for the coaching to take place rather than formalising

accidental coaching can be a high-risk strategy

any direct approach and managing the journey. Unless you have a high level of trust in the relationship, this approach can be a difficult one as there are few visible controls or measures in place.

Typical actions that you will take when adopting an accidental style include:

◆ creating a coaching process that is not locked into time – rather it is based around valuable interactions

◆ placing a lot of emphasis on the client owning the diary – give them headroom to take ownership of the meeting strategy and action plans

◆ recognising that the use of the accidental approach will probably incur 'apparent' wasted time – when in fact it is simply part of the journey – so don't get frustrated if things don't seem to be moving forward at the pace you anticipated

◆ being alert to unexpected outcomes that may be better than the one the client originally planned to develop.

Backstage style – offer protection and cloud cover

This is the high planning but low visibility approach – where there is a plan for the coaching journey but it is very low key. With this style you will need to focus on preparation, preparation and more preparation. A TV sitcom will have hours of preparation just to get a simple scene ready to play. In the same way much of your background activity might be invisible to the client, but you will be helping to create a pathway for them to make their changes. The backstage approach requires you to draw upon all their power, persuasion and political skills.

Typical actions that a coach will take when adopting a backstage style include:

◆   keeping an eye on the client from a distance to get data on their progress

◆   being prepared to act as a political blocker or backer if you see organisational forces about to act against them

◆   using trigger points to kick action off with the client and then fading back and letting them take it and run

◆   allowing them to get the credit for outcomes

◆   establishing subtle but defined checkpoint measures to ensure they are on track with the change process.

Control style – give them structure

With this style you will be taking a higher level of control over the process and how things get done. Goals will be made, resources booked and action plans set out on the premise that the change will follow a known path. The change is then the aim of minimising any variance or disturbance in the system. Accidents should be frowned on, deviation is not allowed and failure to hit a milestone should cause concern. This method is perfect for the delivery of fixed outcomes, particularly where the plan is built using logical cause and effect reasoning.

With this style – because the planning process is so visible and controlled – your role is more typically that of a project reviewer. The idea is to help the client set their plans in stone, carry out *help the client set their plans in stone* reviews with them, look for deviation from the plan and then help instigate a correction when things go wrong.

Typical actions that you will take when adopting a control style include:

- defining a management system that the client can use to manage and monitor progress

- ensuring that action plans are locked into place before any action commences

- agreeing defined review dates and ensuring that they are maintained

- ensuring that the client keeps a record of all changes and outcomes

- undertaking a formal end of coaching outcome review with the client.

Debate style – leave space to talk

With the debate coaching style, the key item in your armory is conversation. It is not about building action plans or creating backstage control systems – rather it is a process of deep dialogue where the act of conversing about a topic helps the client to see the problem and solution from a new perspective.

This can be seen in the way that many bands create music together. The endless creative debates may take place in the studio, over dinner, in the pub or just in jamming with other musicians. Different ideas are put forward, played with, discarded and then maybe rediscovered. What emerges might be a general consensus or viewpoint about how a song might feel and what the lyrics should be.

Typical actions that a coach will take when adopting a debate style include:

◆ ensuring that the client has the majority of conversation time – ideally in excess of 80 per cent

◆ developing a range of questioning techniques to help surface issues and ideas

◆ overtly not asking for actions and plans – but instead leaving space for things to unfold

◆ recognising that what is right for the client today might be wrong tomorrow – and being comfortable with that.

The debate model happens all the time but is often not recognised, since it's so natural and embedded in the content of the coaching process. The trick is to keep a natural feel to the debate process whilst helping to ensure that it is adding value and not just turning into a chat that has no real outcome.

Coaching questions

The coaching questions for this approach can be considered using the four style quadrants.

◆ **Accidental**:
- How would you best like to control your coaching process?
- When would you like to meet?
- How would you like to meet?
- What do you need from me to help you manage the process?

◆ **Backstage**:
- We need to establish a plan for the coaching process – what is the best way for us to do this?
- Who are the political people that can help or hinder the coaching topic that you want to address?
- What will help you kick-start the change process?
- Do you see the context that the coaching will take place in changing over the period that we will be working together and, if so, how will it impact the outcome that you want to achieve?

◆ **Control**:
- What control system shall we use to manage the coaching process?
- What action shall I take if I see you going off course?
- What specific outcome should we see along the coaching journey?
- How do you want to record the activities and outcomes of each stage in the coaching process?

◆ **Debate**:
- Do you prefer to talk things over and then think about them or think first and then debate your ideas?
- After we have talked around the various ideas, what will help you to put them into action?
- Are you comfortable with not having any controls in place in the coaching relationship?
- What do you need from me to help make this happen?

By adopting the right style to suit the client's coaching needs, rapport will develop, the client will be happier and, most importantly, there is a greater chance that the client's outcome will be delivered.

The emergent style – adapting to the moment

By learning to draw on all four styles, you can develop a style of coaching that follows the client's needs rather than simply adhering to how you like to operate (see figure below).

The emergent coaching style

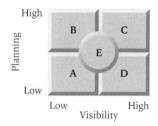

If a team of musicians decides to record a new CD, which of the four styles would be appropriate? The accidental approach is exciting but could leave them using up expensive studio time. The backstage model would be ineffective because only the manager would know the studio time that needed to be managed. The control model seems to be the most practical, but using a planning approach in the chaotic world of musicians may lead to frustration and cost increases as the bass player and drummer fight every day! Finally, the debate model is pretty inappropriate since the group might have fun discussing where to go next with the tracks but the CD will probably take three years longer than expected to record. Realistically, it's impossible simply to stick to one approach – the key is in being flexible, drawing on the different styles as necessary.

the key is in being flexible

Your ability to flex and jump between these four coaching styles is important. No one style is right and also no one style is right for one client. The art of coaching is about the skill of taking a flexible approach to the style being used, based upon the needs of the client, the skills of the client and the context in which the coaching is taking place. Only by taking these factors into account can you make choices about which style is appropriate today.

9

Listen and look for what's *not* being said

CONVERSATIONS ALWAYS TAKE PLACE in three dimensions – through thoughts, feelings and behaviour. To be a truly effective coach, you need to 'converse' at all three levels.

This means that as well as listening to what people say, you will need to ensure you focus on what they are thinking and become sensitive to how they are feeling. Even though you may not realise it, these three levels of conversation are occurring at the same time.

The levels

The three-dimension conversation model, illustrated in the figure overleaf, shows how we all interact and converse on three separate levels.

3D conversations

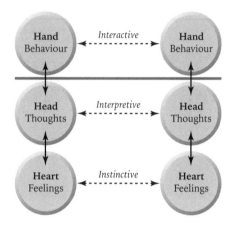

Level 1

Conversations can be seen at a behavioural level (speaking, moving, touching or expressions). You may ask the client to explain their coaching topic and they respond with an explanation. The speech is supported by facial expression, possibly touch and posture. All these behavioural, physical and kinesthetic factors contribute towards a communication between two people. So at level 1 much of the conversation is at a surface or safe level.

Level 2

Transactions occur at a cognitive or thinking level. This is on the assumption that in most cases a thought will precede a behaviour – albeit at a tacit or subconscious level. So we develop an original idea that we plan to communicate to another person or develop an idea that is formed in response to a proposition offered by someone else. Although you may ask the client to describe their problem, they might have thoughts about you, themselves or their relationship with you. These can be positive or negative but until they shift to a level 1 conversation they are left unsaid. When the client responds then you may go through the same process of having thoughts about what the client is saying – do you believe them? – or a multitude of unsaid thought patterns.

Level 3

Connections are those which occur at an affective or emotional level. There is a general consensus that emotional arousal influences cognitive processing. So things like attention, perception, memory and decision making are all swayed and influenced by the emotional state of the brain. This is a powerful heuristic model to understand how 3D conversations can take place between the client and consultant. So we might suggest that the client feels uncomfortable with the current topic being discussed – this feeling might be just a sense that it is not quite correct. They build on this feeling to create a thought that a new topic is necessary and this is communicated through a verbal and physical communication connection. You may feel a response to this action – which might be worry, anxiety or frustration. Whatever the emotion, a cognitive thought wraps itself around the emotion to form a logical response that in turn is transmitted through a behavioural process.

Tuning your thoughts

Imagine you are walking through a busy railway station. You are carrying a heavy briefcase, dragging a suitcase behind you and might well be late for your train. As you run to find the right platform it seems like everyone is getting in your way. You think, 'Why on earth can't these people walk in a straight line and stop crossing in my way?' There is a natural thought that the path you are walking is the right one and the direction the other people are taking is wrong. If you stop and think about it stations tend not to have right and wrong routes between platforms and there are no junctions and crossroads that people have to use to get from one platform to another. Without these directional headings people end up fighting against each other as they try to navigate their journey.

As a coach you need to be aware of the way you interpret what the client says and the extent to which you believe they are taking the 'right' or 'wrong' decision. It is very easy

be aware of the way you interpret what the client says

when a client says 'I want to do X' or 'I plan to do Y tomorrow' for you to think, 'Oh no – that's a bad move.' Although you know it is wrong to impose your solution on their coaching issue, the client may sense what you are thinking and this can impact the choice they make. They may see a fleeting twitch or grimace and immediately retract their idea and decide to do something that is more 'sensible'.

When this happens you have had a 'head to head' conversation. You haven't 'said' that something is wrong and your client hasn't overtly 'spoken' about changing their mind. But a moment has occurred in which the coaching process and outcome have changed in the blink of an eye. We can see this on reality TV shows, where contestants make assumptions about what they think the other person means, and down the pub on a Friday night, where people flirt, fall out and fight – all because of things that have never actually been said.

As a coach you need to stick to a principle that is often called a 'table rasa' or a blank sheet of paper. Try to ensure that you are able to accept whatever the client says without forming a view in your head of right or wrong, good or bad, etc., and instead accept that what they say is right for them – even if it is not right for you. You also need to learn to ensure that if a fleeting judgemental thought does cross your mind the client cannot read that thought. You must be able to display behaviours that don't give away what you are really thinking and so leave the client to create their own outcome and not try to live your solutions. This can be hard as many of our behavioural responses are driven by deeply held beliefs – but with practice you can develop the capacity to present a face that doesn't transmit judgemental thoughts to the client and so affect their journey.

accept whatever the client says without forming a view

If you control how your thoughts are transmitted (level 2) then you will be better placed to tune into what the client is really thinking, as well as what they are saying. You will be able to listen for what isn't being said and help to develop a deeper and richer appreciation of the issues that the client is dealing with. A simple analogy might be trying to talk on the phone while a radio is on in the room. Only by turning the radio down can you hear what the other person is saying. As a coach you need to be able to turn down your internal radio or thoughts so that you are better able to tune into what the client is really describing.

Tuning your emotional levels

You walk into a room full of people and immediately sense an atmosphere. You don't know why, but your emotions have been triggered and you are alert to other people's tension.

Although the neural mechanisms underlying this ability are not fully understood, the recent discovery of a special class of neuron, the 'mirror' neuron, has provided some clues about how people make this instinctive connection at an emotional level. They were first identified when a group of researchers found individual neurons in the brains of macaque monkeys that fired when the monkeys grabbed an object *and* when the monkeys watched another monkey grab the same object. This connection is involuntary and automatic – so we don't have to *think* about what other people are doing or feeling, we simply know or feel it.

The links formed at level 3 (affective), on page 89, may well be driven by mirror neurons. These neurons respond equally when we perform an action and when we witness someone else perform the same action. In the coaching context, to work with this level, you need to develop your ability to tune into this otherwise unconscious 'skill' and learn to harness it. To get a sense of where you are now, ask yourself the following:

◆   Do I have the ability to shield and prevent the client from seeing my emotional responses in case they might have a negative impact?

◆   Can I help the client to recognise their emotional states and how they impact others?

◆ Can I help the client tune into other people's affective states?

◆ How will I help the client to surface their real thoughts?

◆ How can I help the client surface what they are really feeling?

Putting it all together

3D conversations

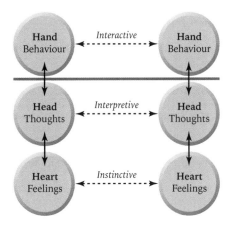

As we have seen, all coaching conversations will take place on three levels. The interactive will be physical and conversational, using words, touch and body language. The interpretive will take place as you think about what the other person means and they think about your responses. The instinctive will take place as you use deep-rooted skills to tune into how the other person feels and how they respond emotionally to your behaviour.

Only by ensuring that as a coach you are aware of these three levels and learn to manage the transactions can you really listen for what isn't being said. If you just focus on the words and behaviours then up to 80 per cent of the conversation will be lost and, as a result, your coaching outcome will probably be less succesful. Some people (often great salespeople) do this automatically – but for many people it is just a case of practising and getting used to seeing conversations take place on these three levels.

Coaching questions

Useful questions you can ask the client to help surface how they really think and feel are:

◆ Can you describe your situation?

◆ When you describe your situation what are you thinking?

◆ Do these thoughts help or hinder your situation?

◆ What do you feel when you describe your situation?

◆ How do you feel when I ask these types of question?

◆ How do you think I feel about your situation?

The more you can help your client better understand themselves, and you better understand them from a non-judgemental position, the deeper the connection you will have with them, and the more meaningful the coaching relationship.

10

If you do what you've always done – you will get what you've always got!

How to get successful solutions

IF YOU ASK A CLIENT to come up with a new solution to a problem, they are likely to try to avoid this, preferring the comfort of tried and tested ideas. Your goal is to help the client look for new solutions to old problems to ensure they move away from unhelpful patterns once and for all.

Beware the client who asks you what they should do

the solution generation stage is often fraught with difficulties

The solution generation stage is often said to be the easiest. But in my experience it is often fraught with difficulties – namely it takes longer than either you or the client antici-pated and often ends up with a solution that has no real creativity or spark. These difficul-ties arise because of the following factors.

◆ Often an overdependence on you to 'give' the answer – this is because the client has come to be 'fixed' rather than to be helped to develop their own outcomes.

◆ In many cases a natural desire on your part to 'fix' the client – this is often because we intuitively think we know the answer and so want to give the client the gift of our solution.

◆ A belief that what works for one person will work for another – the truth is that it doesn't. What helps one person give up smoking may not work for another. All solutions have to be grounded in the experiences of the client rather than the coach.

◆ Often clear criteria are not set out at the start – so clients come up with wildly ambitious outcomes that are way beyond any possibility of what they can realistically achieve. As a consequence they get frustrated once they begin the change and it tends to choke at some point.

◆ The creation of solutions that look good on paper but that the client is not really motivated to attempt.

Examples of problems associated with this stage can be seen every day on TV, where people are looking to move or make some other major life change. The 'expert' runs off and finds three or four places and then the client picks one of these and lives happily ever after. However, if it were that simple then the solution stage would be easy – the client could wander off, find their solution and come back to present it to you all wrapped and ready. The problem is that most problem-solving processes follow a path that is hindered and harmed by distorted mental maps, comfort zone thinking and misconception about what the real issue is. The result is that people often do what they have always done and therefore get what they've always got.

Always push the boundary

To avoid this, in the solution stage you should challenge the client to open up any self-limiting maps and hence broaden the solution they create. You can help them think the unthinkable and find innovative thoughts and ideas that they would not have considered in isolation. In essence the goal is to help the client create great new ideas and explore what they *could do*; to test and validate these possible options to understand which of them they *would do* and want to do; and finally, to spend time helping the client to work out what they *should do* so as to enable a successful and sustainable outcome.

Solution steps

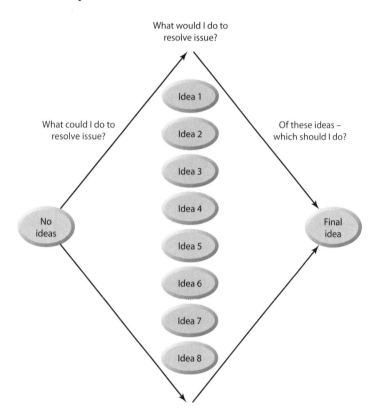

The three-step solution model is shown above.

be wary of offering solutions to the client's problem

However, you must always be wary of the risk of offering solutions to the client's problem. First of all, every solution that you offer is surrounded in a political wrapper. Underneath all coach/client relationships will be an inherent power relationship. You will often be seen as the expert in the relationship and so what you say is seen as the correct way of looking at things. The risk with this is that the client takes your solution and fails to discover solutions of their own. Second, even when you do have prior knowledge, it is experience from your history and might not be fit for the client's world. The fact that you may have had some experience in the area is almost immaterial. In your mind it may be up to date and of use, but it has probably moved past its sell-by date. Finally, the moment you offer a solution to someone then you have created potential for dependency in the relationship. If the client walks away thinking that they cannot solve their own problems then they will end up returning to you to solve the next problem – this can in many ways be viewed as a failed coaching engagement. On top of this, if the solution turns out to be a bad one then the client can blame you and minimise any ownership on their part.

Great solutions are uncovered in three stages

Think about someone buying a new home. They will go through a complex solution process to choose the right one. However, this is something we often do intuitively and without any awareness of the strategies being followed. So, what steps do people actually follow?

In the 'could' stage they will typically define what the problem is and the criteria that the solution has to meet to satisfy the need. For example, a new addition to the family is coming along so there is a need for a bigger house, to be near the school and close to the shops. Within the 'could' stage they will begin to look for a location and property. So, in essence, they will be asking what they could buy within their budget. Once the location is identified they might start to explore the different properties that are available. After the options are listed and the properties are identified, they move from an exploratory process to a decision-making approach. Here they ask which of these properties they would be prepared to live in. They might look at each of the houses in more detail and appraise them for suitability against the original criteria. As they go through this process, they will be (intuitively and explicitly) testing each house against a set of criteria that probably includes cost, quality and suitability. Once they understand which of the houses they would be prepared to live in, the question is which one they should buy. To do this they will prioritise and evaluate the options to make the final choice.

Stage 1 – What could you do?

The 'could' stage of the journey will be driven by two factors:

◆ 'Challenge' – the need to define clearly the criteria being used to assess the outcome (i.e. what will good look like)

◆ Randomise – brainstorming potential solutions, a deliberate process to generate a rich tapestry of options.

Coaching questions

Typical questions for this stage might be:

◆ What are the criteria for a good solution?

◆ When do you need the solution to be in place by?

◆ Is there anything out of bounds?

- How would you know a good solution if you saw it?

- What are the cost limitations?

- How much can you spend on achieving the change?

- What are the quality criteria – how perfect does the solution have to be?

- Forgetting the normal idea, what would be a wild solution?

- What would the opposite to your solution look like – what would be a bad solution? (This is used to create a new way of looking at the situation.)

- If we take one of the ideas and stretch that further and further and push it to its boundaries, what would that idea look like then?

- How would other people see this – what solutions would they offer?

- Looking back, what types of solution have you used before?

Stage 2 – What would you do?

The 'would' stage of the journey will be driven by two factors:

- Explore – consider each of the ideas, testing to understand the strengths and weaknesses of each

- Appraise – assess each one and filter out those that intuitively do not help resolve the original issue.

Coaching questions

Typical questions would be:

◆ How would the idea work in practice?

◆ What are its strengths?

◆ What are the potential problems with it?

◆ How important is it to you?

◆ What would you give up to make it work?

◆ If it went wrong how would you feel?

◆ Is this important to people who are important to you?

Stage 3 – What should you do?

The 'should' stage of the journey will be driven by two factors:

◆ Test – validate the remaining ideas against the criteria set out in the Challenge stage at the outset of the process

◆ Evaluate – finally, prioritise each of the remaining options against the core requirement to ensure that the end solution deals with the problem.

Coaching questions

Typical questions would be:

◆ Of the various options, which make sense to do?

◆ Would your partner agree with you?

◆ Are there any downsides to these solutions?

◆ What resources would it need?

◆ How long would it take to deliver – does that fit your timeline?

◆ Of the options, how would you prioritise their order of execution?

◆ Does it meet the criteria set in the Challenge stage?

◆ How can you be sure that it meets the criteria?

◆ How can you be sure that it doesn't meet the criteria?

◆ Which is the best idea?

◆ How would you rank the others?

◆ What is the worst idea – why?

◆ Which will you take forward?

The use of the three-step solution model offers a number of advantages for both you and the client. First, it provides a collective road map to ensure that both of you understand where you are going on the journey from no solutions to a clear and robust action plan. Second, it helps to prevent deviation – as it is very easy to be drawn off track as new and exciting ideas pop up in the early stage of the three-step model. Finally, it helps the client to take ownership of the solution stage. Rather than depending on you to provide the structure, the client is able to take responsibility for the creation of their solution – which is a very powerful aspect of the journey towards creating a solution that has the ability to be resilient and sustainable.

> *the three-step solution model provides a collective road map*

Be clear what your role is in the solution stage

One of the important choices that you have to make and agree with the client is what type of coach you are. Do you have a particular expertise in a defined subject area (like sports coach, life coach, etc.) and as such tend to recommend and focus on certain ways of working and certain solutions? Or might you be viewed as a process coach – one that has a range of solutions that you call upon and use these in a tool kit to help the client find a solution that works best for them? In summary, do you perceive your role as an expert, providing defined solutions, or as a process consultant, where your role is to help the client on their journey to discover a solution that works for them? (See figure below)

Expert vs process solutions

Neither one of these is the 'right' place to be, as all locations on the expert vs process continuum come with advantages and disadvantages (see table opposite). The trick is to understand what these factors are and ensure that you are at the place that is appropriate for you and the client. In most cases the problem doesn't derive from where you are on the line – rather it is the lack of understanding by both parties of this variation and how it can impact your relationship and the outcome of the coaching relationship.

	Expert	Process
Advantages	◆ Offers the client an easy way to move forward when faced with a difficult issue. ◆ Has the potential to be quicker as solution can be simply offered by you when stuck without a solution. ◆ Can be (seemingly) easier because solution is well practised by the coach.	◆ Gets to the real issues and addresses root cause. ◆ Client owns the change and outcome and more chance of sustainability. ◆ Low dependence on you so easier to break away at the end of the coaching cycle.
Disadvantages	◆ Little linkage between root cause and solution – client might get what you suggest without any real focus on what they need. ◆ Limited opportunity for the client to adapt and integrate as they are having to accept someone else's view of what will work.	◆ Harder to define what 'it' is – what you are actually doing for your money. ◆ Difficult to project plan with few defined milestones. ◆ Can take longer to diagnose and implement solution, with a net result that it can work out more expensive because of the time being invested.

In essence the broad difference between the two parameters of solution generation in coaching can be viewed as follows:

◆ **Expert coach** – views the world as a stable and rational machine separate from its environment. The content-driven 'expert' gains their brand value from the specialist knowledge, rigid problem-solving techniques and prior experience with other change projects.

◆ **Process coach** – sees the client as a complex system that interacts with the environment and constructs its own meaning. There is no single, simple formulaic or static view of how 'it' is – so therefore it is impossible to provide an 'it' solution. Each answer is unique and has to be deployed uniquely.

be clear as to the optimum point on the continuum

Although the expert vs process continuum is key across all areas of the coaching process, it becomes particularly important in the solution stage as this is typically the point at which the client's eyes will turn to you with the 'what should I do?' look. At this point you have to be clear as to the optimum point on the continuum. More importantly, you need to be clear from the outset that the client understands the role and service being offered.

If I have a problem with my car and want it fixed fast then in most cases I will be looking for an expert – someone to come in, do the job and get out fast so that I can go home to have dinner. If, however, I am keen to understand my car in more depth and want to know how to tune it, repair or customise it then I may be looking for someone to help me find the answers and not just give them to me.

This same process can be found with coaching – some clients will come to you looking to get their problem fixed and others will want to understand how they can better help themselves. It is important that both you and the client agree what they are looking for from the outset to avoid any possible confusion.

11

Good coaches help people change – great coaches help the change stick

AS A BROAD RULE OF THUMB, something in the region of 90 per cent of changes delivered in a coaching contract tend not to last, and so the coaching has in effect failed. Hence good coaches help people change – great coaches help the change stick. As coaches we have to recognise that people are human and as such have a tendency not to deliver their goals in the long term. The trick then is not to be surprised at this problem but to anticipate that this will happen and learn to accept that habit regression will take place. Once this is understood and accepted, you will be able to help the client prepare for remedial action that will help bypass such problems and help create sustainable outcomes.

Always be alert to any reversion to old ways

When you start to work with a new client it is normal for there to be a degree of excitement and enthusiasm from both of you. As you both dive into the early stages where the deeper issues are uncovered then a depth of understanding emerges, following this the adrenaline rush can begin when creating new solutions and once a key goal is developed and delivered then we have a cause for celebration. However, when the celebration is over, you need to ensure that what was wanted has actually been delivered.

Holding the gain is generally harder than getting it

Once the goal is reached then life can get really difficult! I would argue that in most cases achieving success is easier than maintaining success. Think about how many people make new year's resolutions, join the gym, start running or make a multitude of suppos-edly important life changes only to slip back into old habits after a few weeks. The key question to ask is, 'How can I ensure that any changes made by the client will continue following my departure?' Failure to consider the issue of continuance can result in a warm rosy glow at the celebration party but an eroded brand six months later when people revert back to their old way of working.

failure to consider continuance can result in an eroded brand

The question always crops up – why is it that good people go back to old habits again and again and again? It seems crazy that they invest their time, to deliver an amazing life change, and then when we meet them a year later we find that the idea was shelved, set back or simply erased from history as something that never happened. But even worse we see the client about to embark on yet another coaching change that almost mirrors the very thing they tried to resolve a short while ago. But when challenged as to why this is happening again the answer might be, 'Ah yes – but this solution is different – this one will work!'

Anyone who has made a new year's resolution may well recognise this endless cycle. It can be found every night in town halls and diet clubs – where people pay their weekly fee to be weighed only to find that the following morning they undo the previous night's good intentions by pigging out on a chocolate bar. So we see this regular cycle of craving for stimulation, the climax and excitement of the action and then the post-euphoric crash as the impact of the stimulation wears off. No matter what the addiction of choice it is pretty much the same circular process.

The whole idea of non-sustainable change raises a number of significant questions that need to be considered when embarking on coaching a new client:

1 In talking to the client – is there clear evidence of a root problem to be addressed (rather than a short craving waiting to be satisfied)?

2 Is there evidence that previous coaching cycles were sustained (and not a case of repeated personal changes that were not completed or sustainable)?

3 Can a clear outcome be defined and agreed?

4 Do you understand the client's real reason for wanting to be coached?

If you draw a no for any of these questions it should raise some doubt about the viability and sustainability of the client's coaching topic. A no for three or more should cause you to seriously question whether the relationship is going to be both successful and

*help the client to
hold on to the gains*

sustainable or whether it is a potential quick fix that will not add long term value. For coaching to be truly successful, you must help the client to hold on to the gains and not let them slip back into old habits.

The coaching process will need to address the struggle between repressive and reinforcing forces (see figure below).

Sticky forces

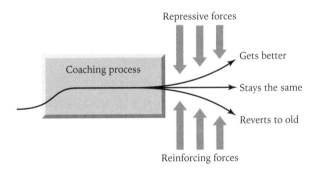

The repressive forces that cause slippage can be viewed as 'buckets' because they describe the impact that the triggers can have on someone who is seeking to make a change. Consider a client who has a problem with their line manager and feels unable to get along with them. They believe that only by dealing with this problem can they get the desired promotion, which in turn will allow them to develop their career. However, although all previous coaching sessions have helped them to develop certain motivational tools, set some action plans in place and develop a new way of looking at the relationship, after a few weeks they have slipped into the same old bad habits.

We can track this personal journey into reversion by looking at what happens on the day after the coaching session. Although they enter work with a personal action plan that outlines their key goals, primary tasks and regular actions for the day, the moment they get into work it turns out that the boss has had a bad phone call from their director and is in a bad mood. At this point the trigger of hearing the boss shout at a colleague feels like added weight that the client has to carry round, and a load that seems to drag them back to the old behaviour of falling out with their manager, thus blocking their chance of putting their action plans in place.

Turn down the forces that cause failure

The extent to which a coaching process will last can be underpinned by your ability to help the client map, measure and manage the negative forces that will cause it to fail in the future. Although the repressive forces will often depend on the content of the client's goal, there are a number of common repressive forces that will cause the engagement to fail to deliver sustainable value.

◆ The client has not been sufficiently challenged in the opening stage to ensure they are really serious about the coaching relationship. As a consequence they embark on the journey only to find that they do not really want to make the necessary sacrifices when under pressure.

◆ You have not dug deep enough to understand the root issues that really caused the present situation. The consequence is that solutions are generated that resolve surface symptoms but do not touch the root cause.

◆ Solutions that have been fed in from friends, TV or supposed experts ('Why not try this new super gym and your weight problems are solved!!') are created that will not resolve the problem. This often occurs when clients think they have ready-made solutions that 'worked elsewhere'. The trouble is that all solutions are context-dependent and can rarely be transported without some form of modification.

◆ Clients often don't like change and so unless you are able to adopt a coaching style that fits their preferences then the chances are that true change will not take place. Real change is where the client is prepared to let go of the old way of thinking, feeling and behaving – and your goal is to help ensure that this does take place.

◆ Only limited measurement processes are used – so the initial process and outcome measures tend to be vague abstractions rather than clear outcomes that parties understand and can talk about.

◆ Flying solo can be a tough challenge – and it is easy to make promises when working together – but what happens to the client when they are on their own and are suddenly faced with the temptation they are trying to avoid? Unless you have helped to embed a sense of self-reliance and inner security then the old urges will take over and destroy all the good work.

◆ The change is not properly closed down and as such there is little embedded learning that the client can take from the journey. Making one change is great, but if the client can understand what helped them to make and stick with a change then that is a gift that they can use in other parts of their life as they seek to make sustainable improvements.

If you do not explore the idea of negative forces with the client, the result is often an engagement that fails to deliver successful and sustainable change. Conversely, when these issues are considered, the chances of delivering sustainable value through change are enhanced.

Turn up the forces that resist failure

Your role in this area is to help take away some of the weight of the buckets and lighten the load for the client. In an ideal world this might be possible, but in many cases once the load is there it can be difficult to erase. Another alternative is to lighten the load by attaching a balloon to it (see figure overleaf).

Bucket and balloon forces

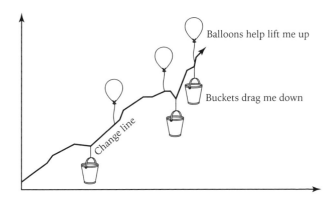

For example, when the client has to present to a management board and they are fearful of what will happen, you can get them to walk through the process and identify each bucket in turn. Bear in mind that these buckets may appear to be fantasies to you but are very real to the client and so cannot be dismissed lightly.

For each of the buckets the client must identify a possible balloon (see table opposite). Critically these balloons must be of the client's making and not yours! No other person can offer solutions to someone else's buckets as they are unique and subjective to that person.

Bucket	Balloon
Worry about mouth drying up	Ensure that chilled water is available
Fear the coffee will be spilled down shirt just before going into meeting	Ensure spare shirt available
Doesn't like one of the board members	Take time to 'accidentally' meet the person in the corridor and chat with them (find their hobby beforehand) to take away the wall of the unknown
Worry that can't be heard properly	Book some acting lessons and practise clear enunciation
Concern that people might think I am inexperienced and shouldn't be presenting	Open the session with statement – 'Thank you for letting me come along even when still learning' – and so get rid of the demon before it can fester
Worry that voices in head will kick in 10 minutes before the session	Arrange to speak with you 10 minutes before on the phone and so create a distraction

Coaching questions

◆ Heart buckets:
  - What emotional triggers make you feel like giving up?
  - What negative emotions emerge when attempting difficult things?
  - What emotions from others influence you to revert to old ways?

◆ Heart balloons:
  - What can you do to improve how you feel?
  - What can others do that might make you feel better?
  - How have you got rid of negative emotions in the past?

- Head buckets:
  - What triggers make you think about giving up?
  - What do you hear yourself saying when things go wrong?
  - What triggers you to think negative thoughts?
- Head balloons:
  - What helps to get rid of negative thoughts?
  - What can others do to help get rid of negative autopilots?
  - How have you got rid of them in the past?
- Hand buckets:
  - What triggers prompt negative behaviours?
  - Do you have any habits that surface when under pressure?
  - How would you recognise behaviours that indicate slippage?
- Hand balloons:
  - What helps to get rid of negative behaviours?
  - What can others do to help get rid of negative habits?
  - How have you got rid of them in the past?

Failure is natural – accepting it is a choice

Help the client recognise that the desire to revert or slip back into old habits is normal and to be expected. This does not mean that something is wrong or they don't really want to change. As human beings we are prone to making mistakes, not fulfilling objectives and sometimes not being perfect – so not always being able to stick to an outcome is a natural process. It is important to surface this issue and make it 'OK' because one of the more difficult aspects in managing the slippage is that clients are often loath to talk about them. In many cases they want to talk about how successful the change will be and don't like thinking that it might go wrong. The trick is to turn the 'fail' word into 'learning'. So in eating the first chocolate biscuit on a strict diet, the client is helped to avoid saying 'I failed' and instead reflect and ask 'What can I learn?'. The ability to do this is one of the most powerful techniques that you can give to a client.

Consider the famous footballer who might want to stop swearing because they are hoping to get a job as a TV presenter. Even once they have stopped for a few weeks they will be surrounded with a multitude of stimuli or triggers that will seem to conspire to make them swear in frustration, anger or playfulness. Common triggers include being around people who swear, getting excited about watching a football match or getting tackled unfairly from behind. Triggers for reversion can be many and your aim is to help the client prepare for this and develop a clear and actionable place to address such situations.

triggers for reversion can be many

To explain the idea of triggers, coaches can reference the commonly known story of Pavlov's dog, which developed associations with the bell that triggered a desire to act. Clients can learn to understand their triggers and manage the compulsion to respond. The trick is to learn how to map and manage the forces that trigger reversion and find ways to counter the forces and so prolong the sustainability of the coaching outcome.

Consider the client again who has panic attacks about presenting to groups of senior managers. They know that until this problem is resolved they are unlikely to be promoted and as such it is quite a significant issue for them. However, every time they try to present they leave the event with panic attacks and self-recriminations.

Although they enter each presentation with a clear plan of how best to deal with the anxiety attack, the moment they get into the room they hear the voice in their head talking about all the bad things that will happen. Although they go on a presenting course, read a motivational book and get advice from senior managers, every time they enter another room the whole lot collapses and they fall apart. This is a simple representation of how a major investment in personal development can be restricted by the repressive forces that cause a slippage back to old ways.

There is nothing like putting on that comfortable jumper that you wear every winter. You have worn it for years and you love slipping into it. One day you decide to change and invest in a new jumper. After a day or two you feel uncomfortable because the jumper is tight and doesn't really feel comfortable and so you decide to go back to the old jumper. It is this natural resistance to new ways of thinking, feeling and behaving that often kills the coaching journey. You must help the client understand what negative or repressive forces will cause a reversion back to the old ways of operating and then, once understood, learn to counteract this repressive force with a positive one. By acutely tuning into what will help make the new way of working comfortable and what factors will cause discomfort you can help the client deliver a change that is both successful and sustainable.

12

Look back and learn

THERE IS NO SHORT CUT to being a truly great coach. However, the one key aspect that makes a significant difference between successes and failures in life is the ability to learn from things that don't go as planned. Great coaches are able to help the client consciously learn from their experiences and ask, 'How was that for you?' To question what value the client got from a particular coaching experience or outcome. So a client who fixes a problem but doesn't learn as a consequence is doomed to repeat the mistake ad infinitum – the client who is able to learn from life's experiences is blessed with the ability to develop and deliver success that will be sustainable.

By undertaking this reflective exercise the client learns to step back and understand better the actions that will help them prosper in the future. It also helps them to understand what they did well and the aspects of their coaching model that were less effective.

LB&L

Look back and learn (LB&L) is a technique to help the client reflect on the coaching process and learn from their journey, and also to help you to understand how you have supported the client in achieving their outcomes (see figure below). Importantly, LB&L is not something that should only be used at the end of the coaching journey. It should be undertaken on a regular basis – either every time a client meeting takes place or when a significant event occurs. In this way the learning process becomes an active part of the coaching journey, as well as something that is distinct and separate at the end of the journey.

Look back and learn

The underlying principles that drive the LB&L process are as follows:

- It is not concerned so much with good or bad or right or wrong – rather it is about learning from what happened.

- Once the client and coach have reflected on what happened it seeks to derive an understanding of why things happened.

- It then seeks to link the learning to the goals and outcome that were set at the outset of the coaching journey.

- Crucially it is used with honesty and openness to try to surface the undiscussable factors that are often buried or hidden in a coaching relationship.

- From this it allows the client to manage their development journey the next time round and also helps you understand how better to help future clients.

- It is different from a de-brief because it compares intended with actual results achieved.

- There are no recommendations for other people as such – but it does not prevent other people from learning from the experience.

You are responsible not just for ensuring that the job is done, but also for helping the client understand how it was done, why it worked and how the client can repeat the same exercise by flying solo. A key component in this stage is the ability to learn from and reflect on what actually happened rather than what the client thought happened in the journey.

The learning process is designed to create a safe space, where the client is able to express freely what they perceived to have happened without fear of being judged by the client for their actions. The suggestion is that the application of a structured and more formal review process can help towards the creation of a more open and reflective learning process. The key factor is that it should always deal with the facts of what happened, how the client felt and what they did and not focus on any sense of blame or judgement.

the learning process is designed to create a safe space

The primary benefits of any effective learning review will be that it:

- creates a temporary pause in the coaching cycle where the client can take a breath

- allows the client to test actual outcomes against planned outcomes

- identifies what to keep within the coaching journey, what to discard and what to focus on next

- captures and communicates learning based on fact rather than fantasy

- allows for immediate fixes rather than waiting for problems to pop out at the end of the coaching process

- signals that the client is serious about the coaching journey and more importantly about owning their part of it.

Clients will learn more quickly and achieve their desired outcomes when they are actively involved in mapping and managing their own problems and developing their own solutions. You need to help ensure that time is made available with reviews and meetings and that the client is actively encouraged to undertake LB&L activity whenever possible.

Tools that help the client to learn

Some clients will take to this approach readily – but others may find it challenging because they are not used to this way of operating. There are a few things that can help with this.

- **Focus on the client and not other people** – When the client is reviewing what has happened ensure they don't use too much 'it', 'they' and 'we' language – ensure they focus on 'I' statements. Get them to talk about what they did it, how they did and why they did it. Talking about a broader context leaves little scope to make direct and immediate changes. An example being, I can get home after work and moan to my wife about getting caught in the rain without an umbrella. I can rant and rave for half an hour – but maybe my time is better spent thinking what I can do to ensure I take an umbrella with me next time.

- **Feedback from you** – A lot of your data comes from how the client behaves in front of you. This can be raw data that you offer back to the client in real time. If working with a client who suffers from self-doubt and insecurity and this was apparent in how they walked

into the room the first time you met – if you have seen
a change in their tacit behaviour there can be value in
giving them this feedback.

◆ **Learning log** – A learning log can be used for a number
of purposes. It can aid the process of discussion and
analysis every time you meet. It can offer a powerful tool
to make connections to previous learning experiences
and it can provide a regular snapshot of the client's
progress with the coaching topic.

◆ **Choice point checks** – Encourage the client to use
choice points as a way to record their coaching journey.
For each significant choice they make the client should
be encouraged to ask three questions: (1) What choice
did I make?; (2) What was the impact?; and (3) If I
had the chance again what choice would I make? By
developing a habit of looping these three questions
the client is developing a habit of introspective data
gathering that they in turn document in the learning log.

◆ **Follow-up** – Every time the LB&L takes place there
should ideally be new development points that the
client should address. If these are documented but not
followed up then it undermines the whole process.
Action points without actions diminish the value of the
process, so it is key that the client and coach actively
seek to follow up all actions and not let them slip away
and be quietly forgotten.

◆ **3D review** – As considered in the 3D conversation model
(see Chapter 3), encourage the client not just to reflect

on what they say, but also to explore what thoughts they have when engaging in coaching activity and then how they felt about these things. By helping the client to initially learn how these three separate parts of their personality act and interact, so they can begin to recognise certain patterns that can impact their behaviour.

The LB&L process might be viewed as both an art and a science. The art is in your ability to create a respectful and honest relationship along the coaching journey so that by the end the client feels able to share their true thoughts and feelings as part of the LB&L. The science is in your capacity to knowingly manage the process so that it doesn't become a random walk or just another casual conversation. It must have purpose and structure if the reflective process is to offer any significant value.

> *the LB&L process might be viewed as both an art and a science*

Coaching questions

The whole process is designed to be simple so that it can be easily used in any situation. It follows a set of five primary questions:

◆ **What did we expect to happen?**
  - What was the desired outcome from the coaching exercise?
  - How clear was the outcome – were there clear and tangible measures?
  - Were the measures understood by both client and coach?

◆ **What actually happened?**
- What was the outcome?
- How do we know that this is what happened and that we are not distorting because of our perceptions or biases?
- What choices were made and what/who influenced the choices?
- How does this outcome fit with the overall goal?

◆ **What worked and what did not work?**
- Were there any gaps between what was expected to happen and what actually happened?
- How would the client and coach rate the outcome against the expectations?
- What helped the good to be good?
- What caused the bad to be bad?
- What alternative courses of action might have been more effective?
- Could any choices have been taken that would have delivered a better outcome?

◆ **What have we learned?**
- What have you learnt about being a coach?
- What has the client learnt?

◆ **What should we take forward to use next time?**
- What choices does the client need to stop making?
- What choices do they need to start making?

After many years of working as a coach I really do believe that the notion of coaching and learning are inextricably linked. Coaching without learning leads to repeated patterns of yo-yo behaviour – much like Groundhog Day where the client goes through the same process over and over again to try to achieve the same outcome. But alternatively, learning without coaching can be a challenge – because without objective support, challenging and guidance clients can so often head down the wrong path. Your job is to ensure that both take place and in so doing you help the client achieve an outcome that is successful and sustainable.

the notion of coaching and learning are inextricably linked

And finally...

THE SECRETS OF SUCCESSFUL COACHING can be found in a few very simple ways of working. By following these we cannot guarantee that the outcome will be both sustainable and successful – but they will help enormously. In summary these ways of working are as follows.

- You wouldn't try to climb Mount Everest in an anorak – so why on earth would you try to coach someone on a topic that can't be coached? Your personal and professional brand as a coach is based upon past success not future promises – so do everything you can to qualify in those people with topics that can be resolved.

- Serious is as serious does. Look for real clients with a real passion to change – and if they are not ready to change don't feed their delusion by playing at a coaching relationship.

- There is only one coaching question – '*So what is stopping you?*' Your role is not to fix the client – rather it is to help the client understand this question, understand its relevance to them and then understand how to frame and answer the question. That is great coaching.

◆ Great goals are robust, clear and the client understands what they will feel like once delivered. So many people frame outcomes that are vague, woolly and have no granularity to them. Where this is the case the coaching journey will be like wading through treacle. Great outcomes create great journeys.

◆ There is no one single style – there are just variations. The more that a coach can understand the variations, learn to flex and adapt their style and use these styles in an effortless way with the client, the greater chance they will have of delivering a coaching outcome that is successful and sustainable.

◆ The trick with solution generation is to get a fix that will give a successful and sustainable outcome. Success can be easy – it is the sustainable bit that can be hard. This is where you have to work hard to really push the client to be innovative about solutions they might never have considered attempting.

◆ The ability to look beyond what the client is saying and listen to what isn't being said is critical. The more that a coach can tune and hone their ability to listen to the unsaid, the deeper appreciation they will have of the real issue and the better chance there will be of creating a real and sustainable outcome.

◆ In most cases big successes come from small changes. The golfer holding the club in a different way, the footballer learning how not to respond to unfair tackles (think Beckham) or the team employee learning how not to fight with the one team member they hate. These are small changes that give big leverage – your job is to help the client understand this and then learn how to push the pause button and change the important choices.

◆ Most people have made a change that they have failed to sustain. The coach's job is to turn the 'I've failed' statement into 'That's interesting'. From this point the client can learn about what happened and why it happens, and then learn to recognise the triggers that cause regression and anticipate and avoid them next time round.

◆ The first gift that you offer is to help them fix the problem and the second gift is to help ensure it sticks. The last and greatest gift the client can offer is to understand how to coach themselves in the future and so ease the dependency on others. To do this you can help them to understand reflective learning and from this learning develop a self-coaching style that frees them of any further need for a coach.

The key way to excel as a coach is not by fixing the client, giving them the answers or getting them to change. It is ultimately about how you can help them to make the choices that will deliver a change that is both successful and sustainable.

Successful people tend to think success first and then deliver success second. Your job as coach is to help the client create and build all the success they want by helping them to think about the things that they want, and learn how to get them. As you help the client to plan for their success, you will help activate their choice muscle – and this is the key to helping the client be more successful.

People who manage choice don't tend to talk consistently about failure, loss, problems, past defeats and not being able to have what they want. People who manage choice think about how successful people manage choice in their life and then seek to emulate this.

This notion that my success today is based upon the choices I made yesterday can be simply demonstrated by the parable of the wise old mule. A parable is told of a farmer who owned an old mule. The mule fell into the farmer's well. The farmer heard the mule 'braying' – or whatever mules do when they fall into wells. After carefully assessing the situation, the farmer sympathised with the mule, but decided that neither the mule nor the well was worth the trouble of saving. Instead, he called his neighbours together and told them what had happened – and enlisted them to help haul dirt to bury the old mule in the well and put him out of his misery. Initially, the old mule was hysterical! But as the farmer and his neighbours continued shovelling and the dirt hit his back, a thought struck him. It suddenly dawned on him that every time a shovel load of dirt landed on his back, *he should shake it off and step up!* This he did, blow after blow. 'Shake it off and step up...shake it off and step up...shake it off and step up!' he repeated to encourage himself. No matter how painful the blows or distressing the situation seemed, the old mule fought 'panic' and just kept shaking it off and stepping up! It wasn't long before the old mule, battered and exhausted, stepped triumphantly over the wall of that well!

What seemed to bury him, actually blessed him – all because of the manner in which he handled his adversity. He made a mental choice to be successful – he chose not to let his emotional fear overcome his logical plan for change and he chose to behave in a way that would lead to a successful outcome. Another mule in that well might have made different choices that would have led to their demise! In my experience winners and losers tend to create many of the conditions that eventually deliver the outcome they anticipate.

You help the client make choices that are right for them, their context and their future. Note this is for the client to make and not the coach. Helping them choose the optimum choice is the key to excellence in coaching.

I trust and hope that these ideas will help you as much as they do me. Always feel free to drop me a line at mick@mickcope.com and let me know how you get on with them. Good luck!

Mick

Index